Battles Christians Face

Battles Christians Face

Vaughan Roberts

Authentic

LONDON • ATLANTA • HYDERABAD

First published 2007 by Authentic Media
9 Holdom Avenue, Bletchley, Milton Keynes, Bucks, MK1 1QR, UK
285 Lynnwood Avenue, Tyrone, GA 30290, USA
OM Authentic Media, Medchal Road, Jeedimetla Village,
Secunderabad 500 055, A.P., India
www.authenticmedia.co.uk
Authentic Media is a division of Send the Light Ltd., a company
limited by guarantee (registered charity no. 270162)

British Library Cataloguing in Publication Data

A catalogue record for this book is available from the
British Library
ISBN-13: 978-1-85078-728-0
ISBN-10: 1-85078-728-X

Cover Design by fourninezero design.
Print Management by Adare Carwin
Printed and bound by J.H. Haynes & Co., Sparkford

Contents

Acknowledgements   ix

Introduction   xi

1. Image   1
2. Lust   18
3. Guilt   39
4. Doubt   52
5. Depression   69
6. Pride   85
7. Homosexuality   103
8. Keeping Spiritually Fresh   126

   Endnotes   151

In grateful memory of:
Marjorie Bristow
Arthur Casson
Sybil Puttick
and Daphne Tattersall.

"We feebly struggle, they in glory shine."

Acknowledgements

I am grateful to Peter Comont, Jayne Haynes, Clare Heath-Whyte, Jonathan Lamb, Andrew Marsh, Simon and Susu Scott, Will Stileman and Pete Wilkinson for commenting on the manuscript, and to Matthew Morgan for his typing.

Introduction

¹Peter, an apostle of Jesus Christ,

To God's elect, strangers in the world, scattered throughout Pontus, Galatia, Cappadocia, Asia and Bithynia, ²who have been chosen according to the foreknowledge of God the Father, through the sanctifying work of the Spirit, for obedience to Jesus Christ and sprinkling by his blood:

Grace and peace be yours in abundance.

³Praise be to the God and Father of our Lord Jesus Christ! In his great mercy he has given us new birth into a living hope through the resurrection of Jesus Christ from the dead, ⁴and into an inheritance that can never perish, spoil or fade – kept in heaven for you, ⁵who through faith are shielded by God's power until the coming of the salvation that is ready to be revealed in the last time. ⁶In this you greatly rejoice, though now for a little while you may have had to suffer grief in all kinds of trials. ⁷These have come so that your faith – of greater worth than gold, which perishes even though refined by fire – may be proved genuine and may result in praise, glory and honor when Jesus Christ is revealed. ⁸Though you have not seen him, you love him; and even though you do not see him now, you believe in him and are filled with an inexpressible and glorious joy, ⁹for you are receiving the goal of your faith, the sal-vation of your souls.

1 Peter 1:1–9

"Don't be surprised"

Two older friends visited me during my final week at university. Both independently gave the same advice: "Don't be surprised if you soon have to face a period of real suffering." I had not been converted for long and was still enjoying an extended honeymoon period as a Christian. I had a comfortable life both before and after my conversion, with very few knocks along the way. My friends' advice was timely. God used it to ensure that I was ready for the harder times that were bound to come.

I should not have needed the intervention of my friends. The Bible itself makes it clear that the Christian life is a battle. It is true that, as those who belong to Christ, Christians are "strangers in the world" (1 Pet. 1:1) whose true home is in heaven. We have entered God's kingdom and experience in this life some of the wonderful blessings of salvation: forgiveness of all our sins, friendship with God our Father by the Holy Spirit, and fellowship with brothers and sisters in Christ. But, although we belong to heaven, we have not yet arrived there. For the time being, while we wait for Christ's return, we must live in this fallen world, with all its sin and suffering. Throughout our lives we will have to fight against the world, the flesh (our sinful nature) and the devil. We are not immune from the effects of the fall; Christians will face sickness, loneliness, depression, unemployment and death along with everyone else. We can also expect to experience extra hardships because of our allegiance to Christ in a world that rejects him.

Our experience in this present world will be mixed. On the one hand, Peter can write to Christians: "Though you have not seen him, you love him; and even though you do not see him now, you believe in him and are filled with an inexpressible and glorious joy, for you are receiving the goal of your faith, the salvation of your souls" (1 Pet. 1:8–9). But, because our salvation is not yet complete, we should also expect "to suffer grief in all kinds of trials" (1 Pet. 1:6).

This book focuses on just eight of the many battles Christians face. No doubt some readers will be enjoying a period of peace with little hardship. If so, may these chapters prepare you for the hard times that will inevitably come in the future. Others will be conscious of being in the thick of the battle. You may be battered, bruised and struggling to persevere in the Christian life. If so, I hope you will find encouragement in these pages to keep pressing on.

Our battles will not last forever

Peter wrote his first letter to Christians who were experiencing a period of great persecution. He could not promise that it would come to an end in this life, but he was able to encourage them with the prospect of a perfect world to come. He reminded them that they could look forward to "an inheritance that can never perish, spoil or fade – kept in heaven for you" (1:4).

An Australian friend told me that people in Sydney find it hard to think about heaven because they think they live there. If we always enjoy sunshine, health, happiness and prosperity on earth it should not be surprising that we want this life to go on forever and hardly ever consider the new creation. But suffering changes our perspective. God can use it to lift our eyes from this temporary world and fix them on the eternal world to come.

That was the experience of a missionary, who had seen little fruit after a lifetime of hard service, when she returned home from overseas. There was a large cheering crowd at the airport when she arrived, but it turned out that they had gathered to greet a popular band. Due to an administrative error, no one met her. In her tears she thought, "What kind of homecoming is this after all these years?" But then she remembered: "I'm not home yet." She still had a great homecoming to look forward to, when she would finally reach heaven to the cheers of the angels and throngs of God's people. Then, at last, she would be with her Lord and could enjoy eternity with him, free from all the struggles of this life.

Our battles can be used for good

Whatever happens, we can be sure that God is in complete control. Our sufferings and temptations do not take him by surprise. In the mystery of his sovereignty, he both allows them and purposes them for our good. Peter, writing of our various trials, encourages us: "These have come so that your faith – of greater worth than gold, which perishes even though refined by fire – may be proved genuine and may result in praise, glory and honor when Jesus Christ is revealed" (1 Pet. 1:7).

It may be that, in the thick of the battle, we are unable to see any good resulting from the hardships we are called to endure. But we are to trust that God is at work refining us, so that our lives bring more glory to him. I believe that God uses suffering to strengthen us and glorify himself – not just because the Bible teaches it, but also because I have seen it happen. Those who have suffered most often shine most brightly with the love of Christ. Many could say with Charles Spurgeon, the great Baptist preacher of the nineteenth century:

> I am afraid that all the grace I have gotten out of my comfortable and easy times and happy hours might almost lie on a penny. But the good that I received from my sorrows and pains and griefs is altogether incalculable. What do I not owe to the hammer and the anvil, the fire and the file?[1]

The poet Robert Browning Hamilton expressed it well:

> I walked a mile with Pleasure,
> She chattered all the way,
> But left me none the wiser,
> For all she had to say.
> I walked a mile with Sorrow,
> And ne'er a word said she:
> But O, the things I learnt from her;
> When Sorrow walked with me.

(from *Along the Road*)

1

Image

¹Since, then, you have been raised with Christ, set your hearts on things above, where Christ is seated at the right hand of God. ²Set your minds on things above, not on earthly things. ³For you died, and your life is now hidden with Christ in God. ⁴When Christ, who is your life, appears, then you also will appear with him in glory.

⁵Put to death, therefore, whatever belongs to your earthly nature: sexual immorality, impurity, lust, evil desires and greed, which is idolatry. ⁶Because of these, the wrath of God is coming. ⁷You used to walk in these ways, in the life you once lived. ⁸But now you must rid yourselves of all such things as these: anger, rage, malice, slander, and filthy language from your lips. ⁹Do not lie to each other, since you have taken off your old self with its practices ¹⁰and have put on the new self, which is being renewed in knowledge in the image of its Creator. ¹¹Here there is no Greek or Jew, circumcised or uncircumcised, barbarian, Scythian, slave or free, but Christ is all, and is in all.

¹²Therefore, as God's chosen people, holy and dearly loved, clothe yourselves with compassion, kindness, humility, gentleness and patience. ¹³Bear with each other and forgive whatever grievances you may have against one another. Forgive as the Lord forgave you. [14]*And over all these virtues put on love, which binds them all together in perfect unity.*

Colossians 3:1–14

When I was planning this book I asked a group of friends to list the ten greatest battles they face in their Christian lives. Many of the answers were as I expected, but I was struck by how frequently I read statements such as: "Concern for how others see me"; "Anxiety about how I look and what I wear"; "Wanting people to think I'm cool." A couple simply wrote, "Image."

I should not have been surprised. Human beings have always been concerned about how we project ourselves to the world and how others see us, but surely never more so than now; image is one of the central preoccupations of our age. Because we will only be able to resist our culture's negative elements if we recognize them, in the first part of this chapter we will try to understand our culture better. Then we will consider the very different perspective the Bible gives on the theme of image.

1. The World's Obsession with Image

The world's lack of identity

Two hundred years ago, and still today in less developed parts of the world, almost no one asked questions such as "Who is the real me?" or "What image shall I choose to project to the world?" One writer has observed,

> In traditional cultures the puzzle of image and identity had an easy answer. The "real" you was a given, stable thing. It was a product of the culture and level of society you were

born into. Clothes, job, housing, lifestyle, expectations were all set for you by Providence . . . A stable sense of personal identity comes from knowing your distinctive role, and from continuity – an ability to see your community, family and place in life stretching backwards and forward in time, without abrupt breaks and uncertainties.[2]

Those old stabilities have now largely disappeared, swept away by the whirlwind of change that began with the Industrial Revolution and has gathered pace ever since. Our identity is no longer fixed by accident of birth. Everything is fluid now; class distinctions and gender roles, once so clearly defined, are blurred. And people have greater mobility. In past generations individuals were likely to spend their lives within walking distance of their places of birth, remaining in the same job or role. But now it is far more likely that we will move geographically, socially and from job to job.

There is much that is good and positive in these changes, but they have broken down our traditional sense of identity. Many people are left with no secure sense of who they are. Identity is no longer a given; it is something we feel we must create for ourselves. That, in part, explains why image has become so important. My image is my chosen identity: how I want to think of myself and how I want others to see me.

The world's lack of security

At times the stability of the old social structures was as a prison. Many, especially women and the working classes, found it hard to escape from their lot in life and a narrowly confined sphere of existence. But the old order did at least provide a sense of security resulting from the fact that most lived their whole lives surrounded by familiar people and places, and engaged in the same occupation. In the modern world the individual is often detached from those old securities. Increased mobility has resulted in a much reduced sense of community and family breakdown has left many feeling very much on their own in a lonely, frightening world. This isolation explains the yearning, even the desperation, of people to be accepted by others and to find a sense of belonging within a group of friends. Hollywood, television and glossy magazines set an impossibly high standard for us to attain. They feed us with the lie that everyone else is stunningly beautiful and effortlessly successful: suave, sophisticated and confident. It is easy to believe that, if we want anyone to like us, we must be the same, or at least pretend that we are.

Our culture's lack of identity and security is a powerful force. It fuels our obsession with image. Our appearance, achievements and possessions, all of which are key ingredients of our image, become all-important. They not only determine our sense of self-worth; they also define who we are.

"I am how I look"

A survey by *J17*, a magazine for teenage girls, revealed that 75% of girls between twelve and seventeen would like cosmetic surgery because it would make them feel happier about the way they look and would stop friends from teasing them. Of the girls surveyed, 33% thought about their body shape all the time. Only 14% were happy with their appearance.[3] Research has also revealed significant changes in girls' diaries. A typical extract from 1892 reads, "Resolved . . . to work seriously. To be self-restrained in conversation and actions. Not to let my thoughts wander. To be dignified. Interest myself more in others." A century later, girls had very different concerns. One wrote: "I will try to make myself better any way I possibly can . . . I will lose weight, get new lenses, already got new haircut, good make-up, new clothes and accessories."[4] Whereas in the past young girls thought of goodness in terms of moral character, now many think first of appearance.

This concern is certainly not limited to teenagers. Naomi Wolf wrote her best-selling *The Beauty Myth* out of her frustration that, despite all the changes achieved by the feminist movement, the self-esteem of many women was still largely determined by their attitudes to their bodies.

> More women have more money and power and scope and legal recognition than we have ever had before; but in terms of how we feel about ourselves physically, we may actually be worse off than our unliberated grandmothers. Recent research consistently shows that inside the majority of the West's controlled, attractive, successful working women, there is a secret "underlife" poisoning our freedom; enthused with notions of beauty, it is a dark vein of self-hatred, physical obsessions, terror of aging, and dread of lost-control.[5]

We should not think that the obsession with image is an exclusively feminine preserve. A recent survey of fifteen-year-old boys revealed that they worry about their looks as much as girls do. Only 13% were happy with their bodies, and 84% believed better bodies would improve their lives. They said that pressure from girls (42%), celebrity pictures (28%) and comments from other boys

(24%) led to their loss of self-esteem. A majority (60%) worry about their body shape at least twice a week; 28% do so every day.[6]

Many men do not leave those anxieties behind as they get older. The market for men's grooming products has grown exponentially in recent years. One leading cosmetic surgery clinic reported in 2005 that the proportion of male clients grew from 5% to 20% in the previous three years.[7] More and more men are joining gyms, driven not just by the need to get fit but also by a desire to look good. It is surely no coincidence that these increases coincide with the more frequent appearance of semi-naked men showing off their toned bodies in magazines and films. Naomi Wolf has commented: "Advertisers have recently figured out that undermining sexual self-confidence works whatever the targeted gender . . . men are now looking at mirrors instead of at girls."[8]

"I am what I eat"

Our concern for the body and appearance leads in turn to a preoccupation with food. When seven thousand women responded to a questionnaire in *Cosmopolitan* magazine in 1994, 66% admitted to thinking about food a lot or all of the time and 25% said they were always on a diet. Of the dieters, 14% kept their weight down using laxatives, another 14% by vomiting and 7% used appetite suppressants.[9] Some of those women were probably wise to seek to reduce their weight for health reasons but surely many others, whose body weights were perfectly normal, had decided they were excessively large based on comparisons with the models and movie stars who fill our magazines and screens. Dieters often set themselves unrealistic weight-loss goals and then suffer a great sense of failure and loss of self-esteem when they are unable to meet them. The result is untold misery and sometimes, sadly, physical and psychological illness. It is not only women who suffer. Although the majority of those affected by anorexia and bulimia are female, there has been a gradual increase in male sufferers in recent years.

"I am what I wear"

The way we think about clothes also reflects our concern for our appearance. Clothes once reflected an identity that was already fixed. People wore what everyone else wore in their profession or station of life. Now, increasingly, clothes have become a means of creating an identity. I can choose who I want to be by the clothes I wear. We can see this very clearly in the fashion choices made by teenagers. Overnight a teen can become a Goth, a punk or a skin-head simply by wearing the appropriate uniform. They may convince themselves that their image is an act of rebellion, but it is not. It is an act of conformity. They conform to the style of a particular group because they are desperate to find acceptance within that group and also to have the sense of belonging and identity it gives them.

In our different ways, many of us are just like those teenagers. Our concern about what others think of us often drives our choice of what to wear. As a result clothes have huge significance for us. We waste hours, even days, worrying about what to wear on a particular occasion. We spend large sums of money filling our already overflowing wardrobes with clothes which we will hardly wear.

"I am what I buy"

My image is not limited to my appearance. It is a package, which I can construct through all my purchases. "The self has become [like modeling clay], to be squeezed and shaped at will. It is a commodity to be designed and then realised through lifestyle purchasing."[10] In my choice of car, home décor, music or DVD I have an opportunity to create who I am, or at least how I want to be seen. One journalist has shrewdly observed:

> Consumerism is the primary force shaping our culture today. It is the force that makes us buy things not because we need them, but because they give us an identity and are a symbol of who we are. This is dictated to us by the media – by magazines, by T.V. programmes, by adverts, by films. We know what Volvo drivers are like and that they are very different from Renault Clio drivers.[11]

Our identity is defined by whether we drink beer or wine, Pepsi or Coke; use a PC or a Macintosh; read *The Times* or the tabloids; listen to Chopin or Coldplay; and go camping or cruising.

"I am what I do"

Our occupation also determines how we view ourselves and how others view us. Our instinctive scale quickly ranks someone else above or below us. Most of us want to get as far up the scale as possible and be a success in the world of work. Sometimes without realizing it, we bring the same mentality into church life. It becomes important for us to be entrusted with particular responsibilities – not to enable us to better serve Christ and his people, but so we can establish a respected position. Sadly, our motivations even for Christian work can be tainted by this desire to get ahead of others.

The desire to succeed is all-important for some. Former heavyweight boxing champion Floyd Paterson brought a bag full of disguises to every fight. If, after the fight, he could not leave the locker room as a winner, at least he could leave as another person. Losing was unthinkable.[12] The same is true for all those who find their identity in their work: the student who works under constant pressure to achieve those grades; the mother who frantically tries to be superwoman: doing a full-time job, running around after the kids, keeping the house spotless and looking great herself; or the employee who works incessantly and may even sacrifice moral values or relationships in pursuit of a promotion.

What we then see

Our view of ourselves

Our culture's obsession with image is bound to have an effect on all of us. It is hardly surprising that our sense of identity and security is often so fragile, for if it is bound up with our appearance, what happens when we grow old and our bodies decay? "Every new wrinkle, pound gained or grey hair is a minor tragedy."[13] "If self-image is rooted in nothing deeper than a well-presented image and the affirmation received from others, it is easily destroyed . . . A *faux-pas* in your choice of [shoes] can mean a collapsed sense of personal worth."[14] And if everything depends on me being successful, what happens when I fail?

Our view of others

We almost unconsciously adopt a consumer mentality, even in our approach to people. We view our relationships with others chiefly in terms of how they will enhance (or tarnish) our image. So we look to associate with the beautiful people, the in-crowd. And we avoid others, because being seen with them might not be good for our "street-cred." Our friends, children, even our spouse, become useful accessories to improve our image.

Our view of God

The more we allow ourselves to be infected by the world's mentality, the further we will drift from God. We must face the reality that wholehearted commitment to Christ will not be good for our image. We follow Jesus, who was "despised and rejected by men" (Isa. 53:3). It is impossible to live both for Jesus and our image. The letter of James in the New Testament presents us with a stark choice: "You adulterous people, don't you know that friendship with the world is hatred toward God? Anyone who chooses to be a friend of the world becomes an enemy of God" (Jas. 4:4).

2. God's Gift of a New Identity in Christ

God's gracious gift

Ultimately we find our identity and security in God and our relationship with him. Although our lack of a sense of who we are in Christ may have become more pronounced in recent years because of a range of cultural factors, it is not a modern phenomenon. Our distancing ourselves from God dates back to the fall. We lost our true identity and security the moment we turned away from God. Ever since, we have tried to fill the gap by our own efforts. We have sought to recover our lost identity and find acceptance and security on our own, without any help from God. But weight loss and exercise, chic lifestyles and working our way up the academic or career ladder will never work; we cannot save ourselves. Our only hope lies in God. If we are to be free from the world's obsession with image we must stop focusing on what we seek to create for ourselves and look instead to God and what he alone can give us. We can never find our true identity; we can only receive it in Christ as a gift of God's grace.

A new status

In his letter to the Colossians, Paul counters false teachers who had been unsettling believers. At the beginning of chapter three, the section that appears at the beginning of this chapter, the apostle focuses on Christian living. The false teachers were legalistic. They urged people to obey a whole series of rules and regulations that went way beyond the principles of Scripture: "Do not handle! Do not taste! Do not touch!" (2:21). Their twisted logic led them to believe that their relationship with God depended on what they did for him. Paul, by contrast, insists that our acceptance by God depends not on what we do for him, but on what he has done for us in Christ. We are not called to live a life of holiness in order to secure God's approval. Through Christ, Christian believers already have a new status as those who are fully right with God. That new identity, graciously given by God in Christ, is the basis from which Paul makes his appeal to us to live godly lives.

This is not the place for an exposition of the whole of Colossians 3:1–14. Our focus will be on what that passage teaches about our new identity in Christ. All Christian believers have been raised with Christ and are being renewed like Christ.

Raised with Christ

> Since, then, you have been raised with Christ, set your hearts on things above, where Christ is seated at the right hand of God. Set your minds on things above, not on earthly things. For you died, and your life is now hidden with Christ in God. When Christ, who is your life, appears, then you also will appear with him in glory.
>
> Colossians 3:1–4

Christians do not have to search for an identity; we have been given one in Christ. The most important fact about me is not that I am British or Chinese, black or white, single or married, heterosexual or homosexual, a builder or a ballerina. Above all, I am a Christian. In words Paul once used of himself, I am "a man in Christ" (2 Cor. 12:2).

A crowd always gathers around a new baby when the parents first bring him or her to church. I try to be a good pastor and join in the welcome by saying, "Isn't she lovely! What's her name?" The father inevitably replies rather frostily, "His name is John." Someone may then do their best to recover the situation and ask, "Is this his first Sunday in church?" The parents say, "Yes, he was only born on Monday," but it could be argued that the baby has in fact been coming to church for the last nine months. He is united to his mother in the womb. Wherever she goes, he goes with her; and if we have put our trust in Christ, we are in him. What has happened to him has happened to us.

The expression "in Christ" appears 164 times in Paul's letters. It speaks of being united to and bound up with him. That is the reality that lies behind Paul's words in Colossians 3:1–4. We have "died with Christ" (2:20; 3:3), been "raised with Christ" (3:1) and, when he returns, we "will appear with him in glory" (3:4).

As a result of our union with Christ, his death and resurrection are no longer simply historical facts. They are events in which we have participated and which have enormous implications for us in the present. We are new people. As far as God is concerned the old me, my sinful nature, is gone and I have received new life through faith in Christ. I have been raised with him. As Paul writes to the Corinthians: "if anyone is in Christ, he is a new creation; the old has gone, the new has come!" (2 Cor. 5:17).

What we then see

Our view of ourselves

These great truths should profoundly affect the way we view ourselves. Perhaps we have a low self-image. We are very conscious that we are single, divorced, adopted, disabled, or that in some other way we do not conform to our own idea of perfection. Those realities may have a significant bearing on our lives, but they are not nearly as important as our relationship with Christ. Our identity is not found in our marital status, race, job or state of health; it is found in Christ.

As I grow in understanding of the reality and security of my new identity in Christ I will increasingly be set free from the world's obsession with image. I do not

have to keep chasing after the acceptance of others; the
Creator of the universe has already accepted me. I am set
free from bondage to the opinions of my peers. I do not
have to conform to a particular shape, follow an expected career path or wear the latest fashions; God has
accepted me and loves me as I am.

Our view of others

We must apply the crucial significance of our identity in
Christ not just to how we think about ourselves, but also
to our attitude to those we love in the next generation.
Christian parents too often share the worldly aspirations
of their non-Christian friends for their children. Many
seem to care more that they gain the right qualifications,
find a respectable job, settle in a comfortable area, marry
and raise a family than that they know Christ and grow in
knowledge and love of him. But, in the Bible's perspective, it does not ultimately matter whether a person is
married, drives a Mercedes, lives in a mansion and is a
millionaire managing director; or is a bachelor who drives
a banged-up car, lives in a bungalow and is a broke but-
cher. But it is of infinite importance that we are in Christ
and can look forward to spending eternity with him.

Renewed like Christ

> Do not lie to each other, since you have taken off your old
> self with its practices and have put on the new self, which
> is being renewed in knowledge in the image of its Creator.
> Colossians 3:9–10

Some people get the impression that if they become
Christians their personalities will wither and they will

become less human. That explains one magazine's urgent warning to new students that they should avoid any attempt by Christians to evangelize them: "DO NOT SUCCUMB! Remember that it is better to be the most horrible, friendless, despised atheist on the planet than it is to be the world's most popular Christian."[15]

But Christ makes us *more* human, not less. The human race was created "in God's image" (Gen. 1:27) to reflect his glory by our likeness to him. That image was marred by human rebellion against God at the fall and so we are no longer the people we were designed to be. But, in his great love, God was so determined to restore us that he sent his Son Jesus to be our Savior. He is the perfect man: "the image of the invisible God" (Col. 1:15). Although he lived a blameless life and did not deserve to die, he faced the penalty of death in the place of sinners. As a result, it is now possible for us to be new people through faith in him. We have "taken off" our "old self" and "put on the new self." We have a new identity in God's eyes: no longer as sinful people, but as those who are perfectly righteous before him. That is certainly not because of any righteousness in ourselves; it is entirely because of Christ.

Now, by the Spirit, God is committed to changing us so that our behavior increasingly fits our new identity. He makes us more like Christ and therefore more the people we were created to be: "renewed . . . in the image of [our] Creator" (Col. 3:10). That process will only be complete after Christ's return when "we shall be like him, for we shall see him as he is" (1 Jn. 3:2), but it has already begun in this life.

When each sport begins a new season, there are always high-profile players who have gone to play for different teams. They can no longer go out to play in their old clothes; they must wear the uniform of their new team. In a similar way, as those who now belong to Christ, we must change. Paul appeals to us, "Therefore, as God's chosen people, holy and dearly loved, clothe yourselves with compassion, kindness, humility, gentleness and patience" (Col. 3:12). Our old sinful ways are no longer appropriate; as Christ's people we must live Christ's way. God's overriding goal for our lives is that we should become more like his Son. That has been his plan from eternity: "those God foreknew he also predestined to be conformed to the likeness of his Son, that he might be the firstborn among many brothers" (Rom. 8:29).

God's priority for our lives

These truths challenge our priorities. We Christians too often copy those around us in their concern to construct an identity to present to the world. We share their obsession with physical appearance, dieting, fashion, lifestyle purchasing, career and all the other ingredients of the fluid, fragile pseudo-self we call "image." But Christians are called to live with a different mindset. We are not to create our own identity, but are called rather to receive a new identity in Christ. We are not to construct our own image, but rather to cooperate with God in his great work of restoring us to his image.

John Stott has been a faithful preacher for many years. He has written, "I am sometimes asked, perhaps in a newspaper, radio or television interview, whether at my age I have any ambitions left. I always now reply: 'Yes, my overriding ambition is (and I trust, will be until I die) that I may become a bit more like Christ.' "[16] That is a longing all Christians should share. Whether or not I fit the Hollywood image is of no real significance; but it is vitally important that I grow in God's image. Perhaps I do not reflect the current ideal the world says I should conform to. I am too fat or too thin; my nose is too long or too stubby; I am too tall or too short. So what! What matters is that I reflect God.

2

Lust

¹*In the spring, at the time when kings go off to war, David sent Joab out with the king's men and the whole Israelite army. They destroyed the Ammonites and besieged Rabbah. But David remained in Jerusalem.*

²*One evening David got up from his bed and walked around on the roof of the palace. From the roof he saw a woman bathing. The woman was very beautiful,* ³*and David sent someone to find out about her. The man said, "Isn't this Bathsheba, the daughter of Eliam and the wife of Uriah the Hittite?"* ⁴*Then David sent messengers to get her. She came to him, and he slept with her. (She had purified herself from her uncleanness.) Then she went back home.* ⁵*The woman conceived and sent word to David, saying, "I am pregnant."*

⁶*So David sent this word to Joab: "Send me Uriah the Hittite." And Joab sent him to David.* ⁷*When Uriah came to him, David asked him how Joab was, how the soldiers were and how the war was going.* ⁸*Then David said to Uriah, "Go down to your house and wash your feet." So Uriah left the palace, and a gift from the king was sent after him.* ⁹*But Uriah slept at the entrance to the palace with all his master's servants and did not go down to his house.*

[10]*When David was told, "Uriah did not go home," he asked him, "Haven't you just come from a distance? Why didn't you go home?"*

[11]*Uriah said to David, "The ark and Israel and Judah are staying in tents, and my master Joab and my lord's men are camped in the open fields. How could I go to my house to eat and drink and lie with my wife? As surely as you live, I will not do such a thing!"*

[12]*Then David said to him, "Stay here one more day, and tomorrow I will send you back." So Uriah remained in Jerusalem that day and the next.* [13]*At David's invitation, he ate and drank with him, and David made him drunk. But in the evening Uriah went out to sleep on his mat among his master's servants; he did not go home.*

[14]*In the morning David wrote a letter to Joab and sent it with Uriah.* [15]*In it he wrote, "Put Uriah in the front line where the fighting is fiercest. Then withdraw from him so he will be struck down and die."*

[16]*So while Joab had the city under siege, he put Uriah at a place where he knew the strongest defenders were.* [17]*When the men of the city came out and fought against Joab, some of the men in David's army fell; moreover, Uriah the Hittite died.*

[18]*Joab sent David a full account of the battle.* [19]*He instructed the messenger: "When you have finished giving the king this account of the battle,* [20]*the king's anger may flare up, and he may ask you, 'Why did you get so close to the city to fight? Didn't you know they would shoot arrows from the wall?* [21]*Who killed Abimelech son of Jerub-Besheth? Didn't a woman throw an upper millstone on him from the wall, so that he died in Thebez? Why did you get so close to the wall?' If he asks you this, then say to him, 'Also, your servant Uriah the Hittite is dead.'"*

²²*The messenger set out, and when he arrived he told David every-thing Joab had sent him to say.* ²³*The messenger said to David, "The men overpowered us and came out against us in the open, but we drove them back to the entrance to the city gate.* ²⁴*Then the archers shot arrows at your servants from the wall, and some of the king's men died. Moreover, your servant Uriah the Hittite is dead."*

²⁵*David told the messenger, "Say this to Joab: 'Don't let this upset you; the sword devours one as well as another. Press the attack against the city and destroy it.' Say this to encourage Joab."*

²⁶*When Uriah's wife heard that her husband was dead, she mourned for him.* ²⁷*After the time of mourning was over, David had her brought to his house, and she became his wife and bore him a son. But the thing David had done displeased the LORD.*

¹*The LORD sent Nathan to David. When he came to him, he said, "There were two men in a certain town, one rich and the other poor.* ²*The rich man had a very large number of sheep and cattle,* ³*but the poor man had nothing except one little ewe lamb he had bought. He raised it, and it grew up with him and his children. It shared his food, drank from his cup and even slept in his arms. It was like a daughter to him.*

⁴*"Now a traveler came to the rich man, but the rich man refrained from taking one of his own sheep or cattle to prepare a meal for the traveler who had come to him. Instead, he took the ewe lamb that belonged to the poor man and prepared it for the one who had come to him."*

⁵*David burned with anger against the man and said to Nathan, "As surely as the LORD lives, the man who did this deserves to die!* ⁶*He must pay for that lamb four times over, because he did such a thing and had no pity."*

⁷Then Nathan said to David, "You are the man! This is what the LORD, the God of Israel, says: 'I anointed you king over Israel, and I delivered you from the hand of Saul. ⁸I gave your master's house to you, and your master's wives into your arms. I gave you the house of Israel and Judah. And if all this had been too little, I would have given you even more. ⁹Why did you despise the word of the LORD by doing what is evil in his eyes? You struck down Uriah the Hittite with the sword and took his wife to be your own. You killed him with the sword of the Ammonites. ¹⁰Now, therefore, the sword will never depart from your house, because you despised me and took the wife of Uriah the Hittite to be your own.'

¹¹"This is what the LORD says: 'Out of your own household I am going to bring calamity upon you. Before your very eyes I will take your wives and give them to one who is close to you, and he will lie with your wives in broad daylight. ¹²You did it in secret, but I will do this thing in broad daylight before all Israel.'"

¹³Then David said to Nathan, "I have sinned against the LORD."

Nathan replied, "The LORD has taken away your sin. You are not going to die. ¹⁴But because by doing this you have made the enemies of the LORD show utter contempt, the son born to you will die."

2 Samuel 11:1 – 12:14

A battle for us all

I am making two assumptions as I begin this chapter. The first is that this subject of lust is one in which we all have a keen interest. Our sexuality is a very private part of our lives which we do not often discuss. We can find it hard to believe, therefore, that others experience such powerful desires as we do. But lust is, of course, common to us all – even if the precise nature of our struggles and temptations varies.

My second assumption is that we all feel that we are failures in this area. For many, especially men, this is the battle they are most conscious of in the Christian life, and the one in which they feel at their weakest. For that reason some readers will, no doubt, have turned straight to this chapter of the book. If you are looking for a few simple instructions that will enable you to conquer sexual temptation once and for all, you will be disappointed, but I trust that what follows will renew your resolve to engage in the fight and give you hope that real progress can be made.

What is lust?

We must not make the mistake of equating all sexual desire with lust. God designed us as sexual beings with sexual feelings, so we should not be embarrassed or feel guilty about our sexuality. Sex is a good part of God's creation for which we should give him thanks; none of us would be here without it! Sex first appears at the very beginning of the Bible. After creating both man and woman in his image (Gen. 1:27), God commands them: "Be fruitful and increase in number" (1:28). Chapter 2 of Genesis makes it clear that the God-ordained context for sex and procreation is marriage: "For this reason a man will leave his father and mother and be united to his wife, and they will become one flesh" (2:24).

God, our loving Creator, gave us our sexual desires so that men and women would be drawn to a committed relationship with one another in marriage and, if it is his will, produce children. So if we have a strong desire for sex and experience a powerful attraction to someone of the opposite sex, that is not lust; it is natural. It is the way God made us. But that does not mean we should affirm every sexual desire we experience within us. God's original perfect creation was spoiled by human sin at the fall. As a result, every part of us has been corrupted, including our sexuality, which is now yet another part of God's creation design through which we can also express our sinful desires. Those corrupted desires are the substance of lust.

One helpful book on the subject defines lust as: "Craving sexually what God has forbidden . . . to lust is to want what you don't have and weren't meant to have. Lust goes beyond attraction, an appreciation of beauty, or even a healthy desire for sex . . . Lust wants to go outside God's guidelines to find satisfaction."[17] It is about me: my desires and satisfaction; the other person is often incidental. But, in God's creation design, sex in marriage should be self-giving and focused on the other person.

Our sinful desires are very strong in this area and at times it can feel almost impossible to resist them. The battle is especially hard because the world around us tells us not to bother to fight. Do you want to sleep with your boyfriend or girlfriend? "Go for it!" says the world. "Everyone does it: it's only natural." Are you drawn to pornography, in magazines and on the internet? "There's no harm in it," says the world. "You can do what you like in private." Do you have homosexual desires? "Act on them," says the world. "Accept who you are. Be yourself." Are you married and finding yourself strongly drawn to someone else? "So be it," says the world. "Faithfulness may be the ideal, but it doesn't always work. You've got to be true to your feelings." Are you tempted to have a one-night stand? "What's stopping you?" asks the world. "There's no significance in it; it's purely physical." By contrast, God says: "Flee from sexual immorality" (1 Cor. 6:18).

A fallen hero

To help us in our battle against lust we are going to learn from the account of King David's adultery with Bathsheba in 2 Samuel 11 – 12. After a false start for Israel's monarchy with the wicked King Saul, great hope attaches to David, his successor. He is chosen by God and greatly blessed by him. By 2 Samuel 11 he has defeated Israel's enemies and is securely established as ruler of the whole land. The ark of the covenant, the great symbol of God's presence, has been brought to David's capital, Jerusalem, and the land enjoys a period of peace and prosperity. David is at the height of his powers as both a political and a spiritual leader. He is a true man of God; we only have to read his psalms to know that. And yet, despite his many qualities and the great blessings he has received from God, he succumbs to sexual temptation. Although God forgives him, the consequences of his sin are far-reaching. David's adultery marks a turning point in his life. The closing chapters of 2 Samuel tell the sad story of the gradual decline of his authority in his final years.

If we are wise, we will learn from this history lesson. It reminds us first of all that we should not place our ultimate confidence in any human being. Even the godly King David had feet of clay. It should grieve us when great ones fall into sin, even great spiritual leaders, but it should not surprise us. No one is immune from temptation. We should pray for protection for our leaders especially, as their sin will have wider repercussions. And we should pray for ourselves. There is no room for complacency as we hear news of a fellow Christian who has lapsed morally, or as we read this account of David's adultery. Instead, we should be thinking, "That could be me."

There are four key lessons to learn from the account of David's fall:

1. Beware dangerous circumstances
2. Don't take the next step
3. Remember where lust leads
4. Listen to God's word

We will look at each of these lessons in turn.

1. Beware Dangerous Circumstances

[1]In the spring, at the time when kings go off to war, David sent Joab out with the king's men and the whole Israelite army. They destroyed the Ammonites and besieged Rabbah. But David remained in Jerusalem.

[2]One evening David got up from his bed and walked around on the roof of the palace. From the roof he saw a woman bathing.

2 Samuel 11:1–2a

Work for idle hands

The author of this account makes it clear where he thinks David should be. David has opted to enjoy the comfort of his palace rather than enduring the hardship and danger of the battlefield. It is only evening, certainly not bedtime, but David is on his bed. While his army is busy fighting, the king is having a late afternoon rest. There is much truth in the expression, "The devil finds work for idle hands to do." That seems to be the issue here. David gets up and has a stroll on the palace roof, and from there he sees a beautiful woman bathing. We all know what happens next.

I wonder: as he lounged on the bed, did his mind turn to lustful thoughts? It can be when we are bored, with nothing to do, that we are most prone to sexual temptation. That is when the imagination can quickly wander into territory it should not be entering, when we flick through the television channels looking for some stimulation or surf the internet to see what we can find. For all we know, David could have gone onto the roof just to get some fresh air and his sighting of Bathsheba was pure chance, but might there not have been more to it than that? It is not difficult to imagine him heading for the roof with lust already in his heart, wanting to be fed with some alluring sight for his eyes. The palace roof must have provided one of the best viewpoints in the city. Might David have gone there regularly at this time of day, when the women took their baths?

Taking precautions

There is a warning here for us. Of course we cannot avoid every tempting sight, but we can do much to avoid dangerous circumstances. When is the battle with lust at its strongest? Perhaps when we have a day off with nothing arranged or we are feeling lonely? If so, we should plan ahead and make sure we arrange meetings with friends. Or do we face this battle when we go to a particular place: a club, bookshop, DVD store or beach? Or perhaps a holiday or business trip to a strange place where no one knows us and we can be anonymous? If so, do we have to go there? Or could we make sure we go with someone else, or at least ask them to pray for us to resist temptation?

There are some dangerous circumstances we can do little to avoid, but we can help ourselves in the fight against lust by growing in self-awareness, so we are ready when the hard times come. For example, the per-iod a few years into a marriage can be especially testing: the "seven-year itch." The excitement of the early days of the relationship has died down and, very likely, there are children who take up vast amounts of time and energy. The husband and wife are both tired and have little time together on their own. They need to do all they can to maintain and build their relationship during this potentially difficult time. That will mean talking to one another when frustrations emerge, rather than bottling them up. And they should ensure they keep having regular sexual relations. Not many people realize that the apostle Paul in the Bible explicitly commands married couples to have sex often: "Do not deprive each other except by mutual consent and for a time, so that you may devote yourselves to prayer. Then come together again so that Satan will not tempt you because of your lack of self-control" (1 Cor. 7:5).

Midlife is another all-too-common time for affairs. A wife can begin to feel trapped in a marriage that has become lukewarm or even cold. She longs to feel attractive and loved again. A husband can feel unfulfilled: conscious that time is running away from him and he has not achieved the dreams he had when he was younger. As the hair falls out and the belly starts bulging, he is especially vulnerable to the charms of another woman who will make him feel young again. A wise couple will be aware of the dangers that come with this stage of life and be on their guard against them. They will never take their spouse for granted but will keep working at their relationship, always looking for ways to express and demonstrate their love for one another.

There are particular pressures for single people. All of us are created with a deep desire for intimacy. The more isolated we feel, the more we are likely to be tempted to find a shortcut to satisfying that desire (although, of course, lust does not deliver what it promises and leaves us feeling even more isolated). A combination of loneliness and boredom can be fertile ground for sexual temptation. If we are wise, we will plan ahead to ensure we do not have too much time on our own with nothing to do on days off. It is vital that we give time and effort to developing and maintaining close friendships.

God designed all of us to be relational beings. The more we find appropriate levels of intimacy in godly relationships, the less we will seek such intimacy in sinful, dehumanizing ways. That will mean striving to develop and enjoy loving relationships with others and, above all, with God. As we grow in appreciation of God's infinite love for us in Christ, we will also grow in our ability to resist the demands of lust. In John Piper's striking words:

> We must fight fire with fire. The fire of lust's pleasures must be fought with the fire of God's pleasures. If we try to fight the fire of lust with prohibitions and threats alone – even the terrible warnings of Jesus – we will fail. We must fight it with the massive promise of superior happiness. We must swallow up the little flickers of lust's pleasure in the conflagration of holy satisfaction.[18]

2. Don't Take the Next Step

Will we resist or succumb?

Perhaps it was just by chance that David saw Bathsheba bathing. If so, there was nothing sinful in it. There is no sin in finding someone attractive or being tempted; what matters is how we respond. Will we resist or succumb?

Joseph provides us with a godly example. Day after day Potiphar's wife urged him to go to bed with her, but he refused: "How then could I do such a wicked thing and sin against God?" (Gen. 39:9). When one day she went further and grabbed hold of him, he fled, leaving his cloak in her hand. He was determined to remain pure. David, by contrast, quickly gave in to his desires. On seeing the beautiful woman bathing on the roof he "sent someone to find out about her" (2 Sam. 11:3).

He should have looked away and filled his thoughts with something else. Instead his glance became a gaze, which turned into a lustful leer. Even then he could have turned away, but he chose to take the next step down the slippery slope of sin. It is very likely he was excusing his action even as he took it. The human heart has a great capacity for self-deception. Perhaps he convinced himself, "Of course I couldn't get involved with her, but I can at least find out who she is. She did look rather sad. Perhaps I could help her in some way. Doesn't God say we should love and care for others?"

After a while the woman's identity was reported to him: "Isn't this Bathsheba, the daughter of Eliam and the wife of Uriah the Hittite?" (v. 3). God is very gracious. Even when we seem intent on heading down a path leading to disaster, he often puts obstacles in our way – we can take these as opportunities to come to our senses, stop and head back in the other direction. Surely this was such a time for David. Bathsheba was a married woman and her husband was one of his own warriors. How could he even think of pursuing her? But, once again, he took the next step: "David sent messengers to get her" (v. 4). Perhaps even at this point he was still justifying his actions to himself: "It's very stressful being king. I deserve a chance to relax from time to time. There's no harm in it. I won't go far with her. No one will get hurt." But any resolves he might have made were forgotten when she arrived: "She came to him, and he slept with her. (She had purified herself from her uncleanness.) Then she went back home" (v. 4). We are supposed to spot the irony of her concern for ritual purity and the impurity of the act. It could not have been described less romantically. There is no hint of caring or love in the exchange. We are not told of any conversation. In fact Bathsheba is not even mentioned by name; she is just "the woman." This is loveless, impersonal lust.

The slippery slope

It all happened so quickly because, instead of resisting, David took the next step, then the next, and then the next. That is almost always the way with serious sexual sin. It rarely occurs out of the blue, on the spur of the moment. Rather, it follows a whole series of smaller steps in the wrong direction. The devil knows he is unlikely to be able to persuade a strong Christian to have sex with someone he or she is not married to as a result of one assault of temptation, so he plays a more patient, subtle game. He does not try to get us to take all ten steps at once. He focuses his tempting arts on persuading us to go just the next step. Then, once he has won that victory, he tries to get us to go the next step again, and so it continues. If we succumb, before we know it we can begin to feel out of control, spiraling towards depths we never imagined we would reach.

Earl Wilson was raised in a Christian home and committed his life to Christ's service when he was very young. He had high moral standards and sought to live up to them. He and his wife did not have sex until they were married. He was highly respected in the Christian world and was a regular speaker at conferences. Life was going well. But, by the time he was in his late forties, he was living a double life. In his book *Steering Clear: Avoiding the Slippery Slope to Moral Failure*, he wrote: "The culmination was a sexual affair and deeper and deeper involvement with masturbation, pornography and even prostitution. My life was out of control and spiritually fraudulent."[19] He faced up to his sin, sought help and repented, and he now seeks to help others who also find themselves on "the slippery slope." Almost all of these people find it hard to understand what happened, asking: "How could I have done such things?" Wilson replies, "The answer is usually found in the description of a process by which one mistake leads to another, with a disastrous cumulative effect."[20]

Lust is never satisfied. We give in to one temptation, saying as we do so, "I'll never do it again." We feel terribly guilty and resolve not to repeat the sin but, having fallen once, we find it is that much easier the next time, and the next, and before too long it has become habitual. We reassure ourselves that at least we will not go any further; there are some things we would never do. But what was once unthinkable is now only one small step away. Perhaps we resist for a while, but after we cross the line it is hard to go back. And so, if we are not careful, by one small transgression after another we head into dangerous territory.

Perhaps you already feel out of control, unable to stop sliding downhill. You know you are in very dangerous territory and cannot see a way out of it. If so, swallow your pride and seek help. Confess your sins to a trusted friend and start on the hard road back to godliness. It is never easy to turn away from persistent patterns of sin but, with a firm resolve, faithful support and the Spirit's power, it is possible.

We cannot avoid temptation, but we can and must resist it. Do not take the next step: don't linger on that look; don't ring that number; don't log on to that site; don't go back to that place. Whatever the temptation, don't do it, however much our sinful mind tries to rationalize the action and tell us it is nothing really. We should be in no doubt that, once the devil has taken us one step down the slope, he will not be happy to leave us there.

3. Remember where Lust Leads

"It was not funny"

The journalist Malcolm Muggeridge once met a woman who, he was told, had slept with the writer H. G. Wells. He asked her how it had happened. She told him that Wells had approached her at a party and said, "Shall we go upstairs and do something funny?" "And was it funny?" asked Muggeridge. "No Sir, it was not funny," she replied. "That evening has caused me more misery than any other evening of my life."

There is nothing funny about sin; it has serious consequences. But the voice of temptation says nothing about what happens next. It offers pleasure now, with no thought for the future. If David had known what would happen as a result of his one-night stand, he would never have done it. First, Bathsheba conceived. David's guilty secret was then in danger of being exposed, so he summoned Uriah back from the front. If he would only sleep with his wife, David thought, the baby could be passed off as Uriah's. But Uriah refused, saying, "The ark and Israel and Judah are staying in tents, and my master Joab and my lord's men are camped in the open fields. How could I go to my house to eat and drink and lie with my wife? As surely as you live, I will not do such a thing!" (v. 11). That noble reply must have caused at least a twinge of guilt in David's conscience, but it did not lead him to repent. He went from bad to worse. David ordered that Uriah be placed in the heat of the battle and, as he hoped, he was killed. As is so often the case, one sin led to another. David, the deceitful adulterer, became a murderer too.

Sin is life-destroying

The devil makes sin appear so attractive. He says to us: "Go on, it will be good for you. You owe it to yourself. It will make you feel like a real man, a real woman. You're missing out on all the fun. If you do this, you'll really live." But that is a lie. Sin leads to death, not life. James puts it starkly in his epistle: "each one is tempted when, by his own evil desire, he is dragged away and enticed. Then, after desire has conceived, it gives birth to sin; and sin, when it is full-grown, gives birth to death" (Jas. 1:14–15).

Sin is life-destroying, not life-enhancing. We can see that clearly with the sin of lust. Sex has enormous power both for good and ill. In the words of one writer:

"It is power to create and sustain community. Power to live in love. Power to know another deeply. Power to express the image of God." But, if perverted by sin, it is a power that destroys. It holds us captive and turns quickly to obsession . . . it demeans human beings, reducing them to things to be used, abused and discarded. Held in its bondage, otherwise reasonable men will lie to themselves and others, turn their hearts and minds away from God, leave their marriages and the children they love, and choose to live in tension, guilt and shame, all for the promise of tasting again the brief, pulsing current of its seductive pleasure.[21]

Sin promises so much, but it never delivers. We know that from past experience; we always regret it in the end. It is important to learn from our mistakes, and David's, and remember where lust leads.

4. Listen to God's Word

God's word convicts

By the end of 2 Samuel 11 David thought he had the situation under control. Uriah was dead, so David took Bathsheba as his wife and she gave birth to their son. David must have thought he had got away with it, but the narrator tells us that, even if no one else was aware of his sin, God knew: "The thing David had done displeased the LORD" (11:27).

This is the first time the chapter mentions God. David was so focused on his lust, then on his sin, and then on covering it up, that he had not given God a thought. When lust takes hold of us we soon lose our sense of the reality of God. Satan does not so much cause us to hate God as to forget him. But, even if David forgot God, God never forgot him. God sees everything. We would surely act and speak very differently if we were always conscious of the all-seeing eye of God.

It is through his word that God convicts of sin, so he sent his prophet Nathan to David. Nathan told David the poignant story of a rich man who had flocks of sheep and yet stole a poor man's much-loved and only little lamb to feed his guest. David was outraged and cried out,"As surely as the LORD lives, the man who did this deserves to die!" (2 Sam. 12:5). Nathan responded, "You are the man!" (v. 7).

It is striking to note where Nathan began when he presented his charge against the king: not with David's seduction of Bathsheba or his murder of Uriah, but with his rejection of God and his law: "Why did you despise the word of the LORD by doing what is evil in his eyes?" (v. 9). For the first time David began to see the full horror of what he had done and confessed: "I have sinned against the LORD" (v. 13).

We need to keep in mind here, however, an important distinction that is particularly sensitive in the area of sexual sin. It may be that you carry a burden of guilt over something for which you were not responsible. Many victims of sexual abuse feel that they are partly to blame themselves. That sense of shame often leads them to keep the abuse secret and makes it harder for them to get the support they need to recover from its consequences. If you have been abused you are not guilty of sin but have rather been sinned against. You have nothing to confess but you will need help. Do talk to a trusted friend or pastor.

Although at times some of us may have been victims rather than perpetrators, all of us, in our different ways, have sinned sexually – and we need to face up to our sin and acknowledge it before God. We should begin by acknowledging that the offence of sexual sin is not just that it demeans us and destroys others, damaging personalities and destroying families; above all, it is an offence against God.

Too often we make compromises. We accept a certain level of sin on the grounds that we do not go as far as many people, and we reassure ourselves that there are certain things we would never do. But God's word shatters our feeble self-justifications. He says, "Be holy because I, the LORD your God, am holy" (Lev. 19:2).

None of us have any grounds for complacency or pride in this area. We all need to echo the words David wrote after his encounter with Nathan:

> [1]Have mercy on me, O God,
> according to your unfailing love;
> according to your great compassion
> blot out my transgressions.
> [2]Wash away all my iniquity
> and cleanse me from my sin.
> [3]For I know my transgressions,
> and my sin is always before me.
> [4]Against you, you only, have I sinned
> and done what is evil in your sight,
> so that you are proved right when you speak
> and justified when you judge.
>
> Psalm 51:1–4

God's word comforts

Despite David's confession, his sin still had harmful consequences. The son born to Bathsheba died and the king's authority began to disintegrate. Even if we acknowledge our sin, the damage it causes is likely to remain: whether this means emotional scars, the pain of a broken marriage, or the temptation to return to past patterns of sin. But, although facing up to our sin will not remove all the consequences, we can still be sure of

God's forgiveness. Nathan assured David: "The LORD has taken away your sin" (v. 13).

David was a mighty ruler, but he was deeply flawed. He could never be the great deliverer king the Israelites longed for: the one promised by the prophets who would not only rescue them from their enemies but also restore their relationship with God. But where David failed, Jesus triumphed. He was "tempted in every way, just as we are – yet was without sin" (Heb. 4:15). He faced the penalty of sin, in the place of others, so that all who trust in him can be sure of complete forgiveness. And so, no matter what we have done, we should approach him with confidence and echo the words of blind Bartimaeus: "Son of David, have mercy on me!" (Mk. 10:48). We can be sure that he will: "the blood of Jesus, [God's] Son, purifies us from all sin" (1 Jn. 1:7).

God's word commands

Having shown great compassion to the woman caught in adultery, Jesus said to her: "Go now and leave your life of sin" (Jn. 8:11). The Lord demands more than crocodile tears. "Godly sorrow brings repentance" (2 Cor. 7:10). We are called not simply to acknowledge our sin and to trust in Christ's death for our forgiveness, but also to live a new life of holiness. God says, "Among you there must not be even a hint of sexual immorality, or of any kind of impurity, or of greed, because these are improper for God's holy people" (Eph. 5:3).

The story is told of a man who was looking for a chauffeur for his much-prized Rolls-Royce. He gave the three candidates a challenge. Each was to show how close he could drive along a cliff's edge. The first, with great skill, drove the car within a yard of the edge; the second managed to get even closer; but the third stayed at least twenty yards clear. The owner then made his decision: "The third man will get the job. I don't want a chauffeur who will take any risks with my beloved car."

God has entrusted us with the precious gift of sex. We are not to take risks with it, asking, "How far can I go?" The Bible tells us to "flee" from sin. That will not be easy, but Christ is with us. He both forgives us for our past failures and, by his Spirit, helps us to live a godly life in the future.

3

Guilt

¹*Blessed is he*
whose transgressions are forgiven,
whose sins are covered.
²*Blessed is the man*
whose sin the LORD *does not count against him*
and in whose spirit is no deceit.
³*When I kept silent,*
my bones wasted away
through my groaning all day long.
⁴*For day and night*
your hand was heavy upon me;
my strength was sapped
as in the heat of summer.
⁵*Then I acknowledged my sin to you*
and did not cover up my iniquity.
I said, "I will confess
my transgressions to the LORD*" –*
and you forgave
the guilt of my sin.
⁶*Therefore let everyone who is godly pray to you*
while you may be found;
surely when the mighty waters rise,
they will not reach him.

⁷You are my hiding place;
you will protect me from trouble
and surround me with songs of deliverance.
⁸I will instruct you and teach you in the way you should go;
I will counsel you and watch over you.
⁹Do not be like the horse or the mule,
which have no understanding
but must be controlled by bit and bridle
or they will not come to you.
¹⁰Many are the woes of the wicked,
but the LORD's unfailing love
surrounds the man who trusts in him.
¹¹Rejoice in the LORD and be glad, you righteous;
sing, all you who are upright in heart!

Psalm 32

A nagging presence

A phone service called the "Apology Sound-off Line" operates in California, giving people an opportunity to confess their wrongdoings to an anonymous ear. It receives two hundred calls every day. One woman who had caused a car accident which left five people dead called and said, "I've just called to say I'm sorry – I wish I could bring them back." A man left this message: "I want to apologize to all the people I hurt during my eighteen years as an addict." Others confessed to a whole series of crimes from theft to rape and lying to murder.[22]

It's not surprising that the service is so popular. Many people try to run away from God and, to some extent, they think they have succeeded; but they still cannot get rid of guilt. For some it is a burning reality that destroys their lives. The head of one large psychiatric hospital has said, "I could dismiss half my patients tomorrow if they could be assured of forgiveness."[23] While guilt does not lead to mental illness for most people, many are still conscious of it as a nagging presence in their lives. Sometimes guilt is a distant voice in the background, at other times it is a piercing scream.

Guilt does not just afflict non-Christians; it also cripples many believers. Some are plagued by memories of one specific sin. They may have committed that sin years ago, but they are still not able to escape from the guilt. Others experience feelings of guilt that are not associated with any particular sin or sins but manifest themselves rather in a general sense of inadequacy. These people find it hard to believe that God could accept, love and forgive them. Their feelings of unworthiness are continually triggered. From the moment they wake up in the morning, they are conscious of the failures and shortcomings of the day before. They live their lives with an underlying sense of guilt, always prodding, sometimes stabbing, in the heart.

"Your hand was heavy upon me"

David certainly knew what it was to feel guilty. As we saw in the last chapter, one day he allowed his eyes to dwell on a beautiful woman as she was bathing. His lust led to adultery and then murder. No doubt he thought at first that he had got away with it. He might have broken four of the Ten Commandments but at least he had managed to avoid the eleventh unofficial command: "Thou shalt not get caught." And yet he still had no peace. Psalm 32 probably describes the period after his sin with Bathsheba: "When I kept silent, my bones wasted away through my groaning all day long. For day and night your hand was heavy upon me; my strength was sapped as in the heat of summer" (vv. 3–4). His guilt was crippling. It had a psychological effect, leaving him depressed. It also had a physical effect: he was in pain and had no energy; and it had a spiritual effect: he felt far from God. But then God lifted his burden and took the guilt away.

We will look for help from Psalm 32 in our struggle with guilt and consider two questions that it raises:

1. Have we acknowledged our sin?
2. Have we appreciated God's forgiveness?

1. Have We Acknowledged our Sin?

Denying sin

David kept silent (v. 3) and tried to hide his sin both from God and from other people. He only came to his senses later: "Then I acknowledged my sin to you and did not cover up my iniquity. I said, 'I will confess my transgressions to the LORD' – and you forgave the guilt of my sin" (v. 5). He should have faced up to his wrongdoing far sooner, but at least he did so in the end. Some people never do, encouraged in their escapism by a society that is adept at evading responsibility.

Sin has become a forbidden word; it is thought to be too negative. A character in a recent novel is close to the mark when he says: "Nothing is anybody's fault. We don't do wrong; we have problems. We are victims, alcoholics, sex-aholics . . . victims! We are building a culture of gutless, spineless, self-righteous, whining, crybabies who have an excuse for everything and take responsibility for nothing."[24] A chaplain once rebuked me for referring to sin when I spoke at a school: "I wish you wouldn't use that word. Couldn't you rather say that we have fallen short of our potential?"

Increasingly, our politically correct culture demands that we not say or do anything that might threaten an individual's fragile sense of self-worth. Everything should be affirming of ourselves and others. The National Association for Self-Esteem encourages us to use affirmations to boost our opinions of ourselves. It suggests we write out a statement such as, "I like and accept myself just the way I am" and repeat it when we wake in the morning and before going to bed at night.[25]

If we do face up to aspects of our character that are not as they should be, we are encouraged to believe that they are not our fault. In our therapeutic society we are encouraged to see ourselves as victims, who are "more sinned against than sinning." There is always someone else to blame. Soon after Bill Clinton's affair with Monica Lewinsky, his wife Hillary said his actions were caused by his troubled childhood: "Yes, he has weaknesses. Yes, he needs to be more disciplined, but it is remarkable given his background that he turned out to be the kind of person he is, capable of such leadership."[26]

Our past experiences, especially in childhood, undoubtedly do influence us significantly, for good or ill. We should certainly not feel guilt for any situation in which we were a victim of abuse. But most of the time, although underlying factors might help to explain, or even have contributed to, our conduct, they do not make us blameless. We must not deny our sin.

Diminishing sin

We avoid guilt not just by denying sin, but also by diminishing it. We justify ourselves by minimizing our own wrongdoing while making much of the sins of others. As a result we can convince ourselves that we have nothing we need to confess. "He's the guilty one," we say. "He started it by having that affair. My one-night stand is nothing compared to that." Or, "Why should I apologize for the caustic comments I make? They're no more than she deserves – just listen to what she says to me!" And, "Those bitter, lustful or angry thoughts are no big deal. It's not like I've murdered or robbed anyone."

There is nothing new in the human inclination to deny or diminish sin. "Cover-up" is not a concept invented by President Nixon in the Watergate scandal; it dates back to the garden of Eden. Adam and Eve believed the devil's lie that there was nothing wicked about eating the fruit of the tree of the knowledge of good and evil; it would make them like God. After having eaten, they hid from God among the trees. But, just as they found they could not escape from the consequences of what they had done, so we will never be able to evade our guilt. David tried, but it burned within him. However frantically we try to push our skeletons into the back of a cupboard, they refuse to stay there.

On our knees before God

If we are feeling guilty we should ask ourselves, "Have I acknowledged my sin?" We must begin with a general recognition of our guilt before God and the fact that we deserve nothing from him except condemnation. We must accept the bad news about ourselves and our sin before we can understand and benefit from the good news about Jesus Christ and the free salvation he offers. We must approach him on our knees before he will lift us up and present us with his gracious gift of forgiveness and justification.

It may be that we have acknowledged our sin in general terms, but we are clinging to particular sins without confessing them or repenting of them. If so, we should not be surprised that we feel guilty. It is only when we face up to our sin, recognize its seriousness and seek to repent of it, that we can begin to be set free from the prison of guilt. We should follow the example of David, who finally recognized his wickedness when the prophet Nathan confronted him: "Then I acknowledged my sin to you and did not cover up my iniquity. I said, 'I will confess my transgressions to the LORD' – and you forgave the guilt of my sin" (v. 5).

2. Have We Appreciated our Forgiveness?

In reply to our first question, "Have we acknowledged our sin?" some might reply, "Yes I have, and yet I still feel guilty." That raises the next question: "Have we appreciated our forgiveness?"

Justification by faith

David's words at the end of verse 5 speak of a wonderful reality: "You forgave the guilt of my sin." The psalm begins with his testimony to the completeness of that forgiveness: "Blessed is he whose transgressions are forgiven, whose sins are covered. Blessed is the man whose sin the LORD does not count against him and in whose spirit is no deceit" (vv. 1–2).

Paul quotes those words in Romans 4:7–8 and says that David is speaking of the blessing of being justified by faith. Justification is the state of being in the right with God. It is not something we could ever achieve by ourselves. However hard we try, we still sin and deserve God's condemnation. But Christ has made it possible for us to be forgiven and accepted by God by paying the penalty for sin in his death on the cross. Since the price has already been paid there is nothing more for us to do. We simply have to receive the free gift of God's grace by faith in Christ. The moment we turn to Christ we can be sure that our sins are "forgiven" and "covered" (v. 1). The Lord no longer counts them against us (v. 2).

It may be that particular sins trouble your conscience. You could be haunted by some words you once spoke to a loved one. You have long regretted them, but you cannot take them back or even say sorry: the other person is dead now. Bereavement often releases terrible feelings of guilt. Or perhaps you are troubled by some fraud, an abortion, an adulterous relationship or act of cruelty. It may have happened many years ago, but it is fresh in your mind as if it were yesterday. However terrible your sin may be, you should take comfort from the great truth of justification by faith. If you have trusted in Christ, all your wrongdoing is "covered." As far as God is concerned, it does not exist. It is as if he says to us, "You may keep bringing that deed to mind, but I don't. Christ has paid for it. I will never mention it again. It's dealt with." In God's sight our sins are forgiven, forgotten, forever.

A glorious exchange

Too many Christians have received the wonderful gift of God's forgiveness without fully realizing how all-encompassing it is. I heard the following illustration years ago, and it helped me to grasp something of the wonder of justification by faith.

It is the end of time and we stand before the judgement seat of God. An angel begins to read from a heavy book. It takes many hours for him to do so and, with every line, we feel more helpless. The book is a record of all the sins we committed in our lives. Eventually the angel stops speaking and God asks him, "Tell me, whose name is on the cover?" To our great surprise the angel replies, "Jesus of Nazareth." Then he takes another book and begins to read again. The account of this life could not be more different. It is full of love, truth, compassion and perfect righteousness; not a single sin is mentioned. Only one man has ever lived like that. Once more God asks, "Whose name is on the cover?" The angel replies, "Vaughan Roberts."

Once we trust in Christ, a glorious exchange has taken place. He has not only identified with us and taken the punishment for all our sins; he has also given us his perfect righteousness. God now treats us as if we had lived Jesus' life. In Paul's great words: "God made him who had no sin to be sin for us, so that in him we might become the righteousness of God" (2 Cor. 5:21).

Obsessive guilt

It may be that you understand the truth of justification in your head, and yet you still find it hard to accept in your heart. Some people are psychologically prone to feelings of guilt. Irrational obsessive guilt is a common feature of depression. It can also be caused by low self-esteem. Christians who have always been told that they are in the wrong, perhaps in childhood or in a marriage, can find it almost impossible to fully grasp that they are in the right with God. If they do anything wrong, however small, they feel condemned and quickly assume that God could not still love them. Such people should not let their feelings run unopposed, but should rather respond to them with the great truth of justification. Instead of repeating the mantra recommended by the National Association of Self-Esteem, "I like and accept myself just the way I am," they would do well to repeat to themselves: "God loves and accepts me in Christ despite the way I am." They could learn some of the verses that proclaim this glorious truth:

> There is now no condemnation for those who are in Christ Jesus
>
> Romans 8:1

> Who will bring any charge against those whom God has chosen? It is God who justifies. Who is he that condemns? Christ Jesus, who died – more than that, who was raised to life – is at the right hand of God and is also interceding for us.
>
> Romans 8:33–34

> If anybody does sin, we have one who speaks to the Father in our defense – Jesus Christ, the Righteous One. He is the atoning sacrifice for our sins.
>
> 1 John 2:1–2

Traveling first-class

The assurance David receives from God of his forgiveness is striking. He had committed some terrible sins, but he was in doubt that he had been completely forgiven. He says with great conviction: "You forgave the guilt of my sin" (Psalm 32:5). He is absolutely sure that God loves him and will protect him: "You are my hiding place; you will protect me from trouble and surround me with songs of deliverance" (v. 7).

Some people find such certainty offensive. They think it is arrogant to claim, "I'm saved and I know I'm going to heaven." But as long as that confidence is based not on anything we ourselves have done, but on Christ's death for us, there is nothing presumptuous about it. I am not making any boastful claims about myself and my godliness; I am rather humbly trusting in Christ and the full salvation he achieved. God wants us to be sure of our forgiveness and acceptance by God in Christ.

I was once delayed on my way to a station and jumped on to a train just before it left. There had been no time to check if it was heading to my destination and there was no one else around to ask. I spent a fretful few minutes anxiously wondering whether I was traveling in the wrong direction before the ticket inspector put my mind at rest. I was on the right train all along, but I enjoyed the journey much more once I knew that I was going where I wanted to go.

All those who have trusted in Christ are, as it were, on a train that leads to heaven. Their sins have been forgiven and they are in the right with God. But not all are traveling first-class, enjoying the assurance of their new status before God. The others travel second-class: while heading for the same destination, they spend a lot of time worrying about whether they really are acceptable to God. That does not have to be our experience. God wants us all to share David's humble, joyful confidence.

Imagine writing a list of all the sins that trouble your conscience and then taking a match and setting the piece of paper alight. As you think about the flames consuming the paper, remember that Christ died for your sins. Just as the breeze blows the ashes into the air, so Christ carried your sins away. That is the assurance that every Christian can and should have.

Don't be a donkey!

David was so thrilled by the wonder of God's forgiveness that he could not keep it to himself. He had been such a fool to withdraw from God for so long as he tried to hide his sin. If he had only prayed for God's mercy and help sooner, he would have been spared much trouble, so in Psalm 32 he urges others to turn to God quickly: "Therefore let everyone who is godly pray to you while you may be found; surely when the mighty waters rise, they will not reach him" (v. 6).

I take it that David is continuing with his advice to others in verse 8: "I will instruct you and teach you in the way you should go; I will counsel you and watch over you." He wants us to avoid the mistakes he made: "Do not be like the horse or the mule, which have no under-standing but must be controlled by bit and bridle or they will not come to you" (v. 9).

David had been like a stubborn mule who did not go God's way willingly. It was only after the bit and bridle treatment of suffering that he was brought to his knees and finally came to his senses. The pain had forced him to acknowledge his sin. Now he says to us: "Don't make my mistake! Don't be a donkey! Don't resist God! If you do, he will have to use painful means to bring you into line, because he is more committed to your holiness than your immediate happiness. Let God be God and respond quickly to his word."

If we have understood the great message of the gospel, we will also want to share it with others as David did. We will urge both backsliding Christians and unbelievers to turn to Christ and trust in him. They will thus avoid great suffering and receive great blessing: "Many are the woes of the wicked, but the LORD's unfailing love surrounds the man who trusts in him" (v. 10).

"Rejoice in the Lord"

The psalm ends with an appeal to the "righteous," those who are right with God, to rejoice in him and sing his praises: "Rejoice in the LORD and be glad, you righteous; sing, all you who are upright in heart!" (v. 11).

If we have acknowledged our sin and appreciated God's forgiveness, we have much to praise God for. We may have to suffer many trials on earth, but we do so in the knowledge that God is with us. And, as those who are justified by Christ, we can be sure we will spend eternity with him. We can sing the great words of Charles Wesley:

No condemnation now I dread;
Jesus, and all in Him, is mine;
Alive in Him, my living Head,
And clothed in righteousness divine,
Bold I approach the eternal throne,
And claim the crown, through Christ my own.[27]

4

Doubt

24Now Thomas (called Didymus), one of the Twelve, was not with the disciples when Jesus came. 25So the other disciples told him, "We have seen the Lord!"

But he said to them, "Unless I see the nail marks in his hands and put my finger where the nails were, and put my hand into his side, I will not believe it."

26A week later his disciples were in the house again, and Thomas was with them. Though the doors were locked, Jesus came and stood among them and said, "Peace be with you!" 27Then he said to Thomas, "Put your finger here; see my hands. Reach out your hand and put it into my side. Stop doubting and believe."

28Thomas said to him, "My Lord and my God!"

29Then Jesus told him, "Because you have seen me, you have believed; blessed are those who have not seen and yet have believed."

30Jesus did many other miraculous signs in the presence of his disciples, which are not recorded in this book. 31But these are written

that you may believe that Jesus is the Christ, the Son of God, and
that by believing you may have life in his name.

John 20:24–31

Tom was invited by a friend to a series of meetings which introduced the Christian faith to those who were willing to investigate. He was very struck by what he heard and gradually became convinced it was true. When, after a few weeks, the speaker gave an opportunity for people to pray a prayer asking for God's forgiveness and for help to begin the Christian life, Tom decided to pray it. He felt wonderful at first; he had a sense of joy, peace and purpose that he had never known before. But now, a few months later, the excitement of those early days has begun to die down. He has found that the Christian life is a battle. He keeps on falling for the same old sins and he does not really feel close to God anymore. For the first time, questions have begun to plague his mind. Is it really all true, or had he just been carried along by a wave of emotion? He does not like to tell his new Christian friends about the nagging doubts he is experiencing. He feels they would disapprove; they seem so certain of everything.

Jane has been a Christian for decades. She is one of the stalwarts of the church; everyone knows her. Over the years she has served in all sorts of ways: on the Church Council, in the Sunday school and as a small group leader. As far as everyone else is concerned, she is a strong Christian, but she does not feel it. Life has been hard for a while now. Her marriage is not what it once was, the children are going through an awkward stage and her parents are getting older and more dependent. She feels as if she is giving out all the time and getting very little back in return. Everything is an effort. Although she is conscious, as never before, of her desperate need for God's strength and presence just to get her through the day, she does not feel that he is with her. Over the last few months she has begun to ask questions that never really troubled her before: "Does God care? Does he really love me?" At times she has even wondered whether he is there at all.

"Faith in two minds"

Tom and Jane are fictional characters, but there are many real people like them. All believers are likely to struggle at some time, in one way or another, with the battle of doubt. We must understand that doubt is not the same as unbelief. Too many people fail to recognize that distinction and, as a result, feel guilty about their doubts and are too ashamed to share them with others. They therefore never receive the help and encouragement they need. But there is a significant difference between doubt and unbelief. Unbelief in the Bible is a sinful decision to turn from God. Someone who doubts, however, may remain open to God and long to believe wholeheartedly but, for whatever reason, finds that hard to do. One helpful book on the subject is entitled *Doubt: Faith in Two Minds*.[28] It defines doubt as "A state of mind in suspension between faith and unbelief so that it is neither of them wholly and each only partly."[29]

Doubt is not sinful, but it is serious. If it is not addressed properly it could lead further down the road from faith to unbelief and away from Christ. I hope this chapter will be a help both to those who are struggling with doubt themselves and to those who try to assist them. We will seek to learn from John's account of the encounter between Jesus and the most famous doubter of all: "Doubting Thomas." Our focus will not be on

Thomas' doubts but rather on what the passage teaches us about Christian faith.
1. Christian faith is reasonable
2. Christian faith is faith
3. Christian faith is vital

1. Christian Faith Is Reasonable

A contemporary figure

Thomas certainly did not initially think there was anything reasonable about Christian faith. No doubt he had been there on Golgotha, the place of crucifixion, when Jesus was nailed to a cross, suffered in agony for three hours and then died. He may also have watched as his master was taken down and then, surrounded by weeping friends and relatives, was buried in a tomb. But now the rest of the disciples were telling him that they had seen Jesus alive again. We can understand why Thomas was unconvinced. Dead people do not rise from the dead. Perhaps he pitied his friends. Why could they not just face facts and accept the awful reality? Jesus, their friend and inspiration, the one they had believed to be the Messiah, was dead and that was the end of it. In his heart he wanted to believe in the resurrection but his head would not allow him. He needed solid evidence first. So he told the others: "Unless I see the nail marks in his hands and put my finger where the nails were, and put my hand into his side, I will not believe it" (v. 25).

Thomas is a contemporary figure. Many today can see the advantages of faith. They acknowledge that it would be nice to have something to live for and a source of comfort in times of need, but their minds will not let them believe. They fear that would involve ignoring the findings of science and committing intellectual suicide.

Others would not put it quite that strongly. They recognize that there is a place for faith even in our modern, scientific age, but it is a faith that is divorced from reason. They are drawn to Eastern mysticism or the "New Age" movement. The form of spirituality that is increasingly popular in the postmodern world focuses on experience and seeks to encounter the transcendent and the divine on the sub-rational level. As far as many are concerned, if faith belongs anywhere in the twenty-first century it is in the soul, not the mind; there is nothing rational about it.

Christian faith is built on firm foundations

Contrary to the assumptions of many today, the Bible insists that Christian faith is reasonable. It is based on solid evidence, which the mind can examine and then act upon. While it should affect every aspect of a believer's personality and never remain in the head, it is never divorced from the mind; it is rational.

Christian faith is built on firm foundations. Christianity is not just a set of ideas; it has a historical basis. We are called to believe the Christian message not simply because we like the sound of it and it feels good to us, but because it is true.

John points us to historical facts in his Gospel. He describes seven "signs": miracles which all reveal that Jesus is no ordinary human being, but is the Son of God. How else could he heal the blind, feed the five thousand and raise the dead? Here in the penultimate chapter of his Gospel John points to the most compelling evidence of all: Jesus rose from the dead. John stresses repeatedly that the resurrection is no myth; it really happened. The early disciples did not just shut their eyes and pretend Jesus was alive; they saw him.

It must have been a difficult time for Thomas. He was the only one among those fervent, believing disciples who was not sure. Had they all lost their minds? A week after the others claimed to have seen the risen Jesus, they were all together behind locked doors. Somehow Jesus suddenly appeared among them and said, "Peace be with you!" (v. 26). Then he said to Thomas, "Put your finger here; see my hands. Reach out your hand and put it into my side. Stop doubting and believe" (v. 27).

Jesus graciously offered Thomas all the evidence he had wanted. Thomas responded with worship: "My Lord and my God!" (v. 28). He did not have to stop thinking to make that declaration. Quite the opposite: it was his mind which convinced him. His faith was based on evidence.

God is not asking anyone to commit intellectual suicide. We need to be clear about this in our own minds, and especially when we talk with others about our Christian faith. The Gospels are not myths; they describe what really happened. Luke begins his Gospel with a striking claim to be a careful historian:

> Many have undertaken to draw up an account of the things that have been fulfilled among us, just as they were handed down to us by those who from the first were eyewitnesses and servants of the word. Therefore, since I myself have carefully investigated everything from the beginning, it seemed good also to me to write an orderly account for you, most excellent Theophilus, so that you may know the certainty of the things you have been taught.
>
> Luke 1:1–4

You may be a Christian who is facing doubts. A range of different factors could have triggered these questions. Most doubts are not simply intellectual but, as we will see later, may derive chiefly from our personalities or circumstances. Whatever has prompted your doubts, make sure you speak to them and remind them of the solid historical foundations of your faith. As you struggle with questions, do not forget the answers you have already discovered. As you grapple with uncertainties, remember that of which you can be sure.

One friend of mine became convinced after reading the Bible that Jesus was the Son of God and that he rose from the dead. He has never wavered from those convictions. But sometimes other doubts and questions trouble him. They tend to afflict him in the morning and can leave him struggling to get out of bed and reluctant to live for Christ for another day. He has now learned to speak to himself. "Is Jesus the Son of God?" he asks. "Yes he is!" he replies. "Did Jesus rise from the dead?" "Yes he did!" "Well then," he continues, "stop moping, get up and get on with it!"

2. Christian Faith Is Faith

"We live by faith, not by sight"

While Thomas believed on the basis of what he saw with his own eyes, we cannot expect to experience the same physical evidence today. Jesus has ascended into heaven and is not physically on earth any more. He said to Thomas, "Because you have seen me, you have believed; blessed are those who have not seen and yet have believed" (v. 29). Jesus is referring here to all those, including us, who live in the period since he left the earth and are therefore called to believe without seeing.

We must be clear about what we mean by "faith." Some non-Christians equate faith with believing the impossible: screwing up your eyes and forcing yourself to believe what you either know is not true or what you have no good reason for believing. Professor Richard Dawkins of Oxford University makes no effort to disguise his scorn for religious belief. He has said, "Faith means blind trust, in the absence of evidence, even in the teeth of evidence."[30]

Some Christians respond to that caricature by going too far in the opposite direction. Faith, they say, is certainly not a leap in the dark. They speak as if there is conclusive evidence that proves everything Christians are called to believe and counters all objections. They have neat answers for every question and insist that they never have any difficulty in believing. But they have failed to take account of the reality of living in this present world. There are things we can be sure of, but there is also much we do not know. We are not in heaven yet. It is inevitable that while we wait for Christ's return and live in this fallen world there will be uncertainties and unanswered questions. We live by faith, not by sight (2 Cor. 5:7).

We cannot prove conclusively, beyond any shadow of doubt, that God exists or that Jesus is his divine Son. The same is true of most of what really matters. We can prove mathematically that $2 + 2 = 4$, but we cannot prove that our mothers love us. I could present plenty of evidence of my mother's love, but you could counter by saying, "She is pretending because she wants your money or hopes that you will look after her in her old age." I cannot *prove* that you are wrong but I still *know* that you are. Lord Tennyson wrote in "The Ancient Sage":

> For nothing worthy proving can be proven,
> Nor yet disproven: wherefore thou be wise,
> Cleave ever to the sunnier side of doubt.[31]

I cannot prove that Jesus rose and is alive. Jesus will not perform a special resurrection appearance just for me. I am called, rather, to believe on the basis of what others saw. John tells us that he wrote his Gospel to provide us with eyewitness accounts of Jesus' ministry so that we, who have not seen, may believe. He tells us,

> Jesus did many other miraculous signs in the presence of his disciples, which are not recorded in this book. But these are written that you may believe that Jesus is the Christ, the Son of God, and that by believing you may have life in his name.
>
> John 20:30–31

We accept most of what we believe on the same basis: what others tell us. If I am wise, I will not believe everything I am told. But wisdom also demands that I do not refuse to believe something simply because I have not witnessed it myself. I have never seen Napoleon Bonaparte, but I believe he existed. There are good reasons for doing so, just as there are good reasons to accept the testimony of the early Christians about Jesus.

Faith tested by suffering

Christian faith is reasonable, but it is still faith. Sometimes that faith may be severely tested. There is much we do not know and understand. Sometimes what we see seems to contradict what we believe, especially when we suffer ourselves or have to witness the suffering of others. Joseph Parker, the minister of London's City Temple in the late nineteenth century, claimed he had never had a religious doubt until his wife died when he was sixty-eight. He wrote afterwards,

In that dark hour I became almost an atheist. For God had set his foot upon my prayers and treated my petitions with contempt. If I had seen a dog in such agony as mine, I would have pitied and helped the dumb beast; yet God spat upon me and cast me out as an offence – out into the waste wilderness and the night black and starless.[32]

It may be that your doubts focus on the problem of suffering. Is God loving? Is he in control? Is he there at all? The Bible does give us some answers; it proclaims that God is there and is both loving and sovereign. But we are still left with many questions.

Some doubt is caused by unrealistic expectations. If we think that God will preserve us from trouble, or at least always give us the insight to understand why he has allowed it, we will soon be disappointed and may doubt his love. But God has not promised his people an easy life. The great men and women of faith in the Bible, such as those listed in Hebrews 11, were called to keep trusting in what they could not see despite great suffering. At times they cried out in frustration to God like the psalmist: "How long, O LORD? Will you forget me forever? How long will you hide your face from me?" (Psalm 13:1). We should not be surprised when we face difficulties and doubts; they are a normal part of the life of faith. Christian faith is faith, not sight.

Light in the darkness

Suppose I arrange to meet an old friend for coffee and she has still not arrived twenty minutes after the arranged time. I do not immediately assume that she does not like me and has only been pretending to be my friend until now. I have no idea why she is late but assume, on the basis of what I do know about her, that there must be some good reason. In a similar way, we can trust God despite what we do not understand, on the basis of what we do know. I am sure that God is love because of what he has revealed to me through his Son Jesus and his death on the cross. And the resurrection assures me that God is powerful and will one day put everything right when Jesus returns at the end of time. Those great truths give me enough light to persevere in the midst of the darkness of this present world.

3. Christian Faith Is Vital

A matter of life and death

Most people assume that Christian faith is the equivalent of a hobby. We may be mystified by another person's choice of pastime, but it never occurs to us that it really matters that they have chosen ballooning rather than ball-room dancing or basketball. In a similar way, our society regards an individual's choice of belief, whether Christianity, Islam or atheism, as insignificant: "each to his own." But the Bible presents a different view. Christian faith is not an optional extra that we can happily do without; it is a matter of life and death. Some clothing advertising an evangelistic mission made the point powerfully. On the back were the words: "No Jesus, no life," but the front proclaimed: "Know Jesus, know life."

We are all spiritually dead by nature, facing eternal separation from God because of our rebellion against him. Christ came to make possible the fullness of life that can only be found in a relationship with his Father through him (Jn. 10:10; 17:3). That eternal life is secured by his death and is received by faith:

For God so loved the world that he gave his one and only Son, that whoever believes in him shall not perish but have eternal life.

John 3:16

Whoever believes in the Son has eternal life, but whoever rejects the Son will not see life, for God's wrath remains on him.

John 3:36

John was convinced that it mattered very much whether people had Christian faith or not. That conviction spurred him to write his Gospel so that they "may believe that Jesus is the Christ, the Son of God, and that by believing . . . may have life in his name" (20:31). If faith matters so much, it follows that doubt matters too. If it is not addressed properly, doubt could lead to unbelief and spiritual death. We should do all we can to help other Christians who doubt; we should also seek to address our own doubts honestly and biblically.

"Be merciful to those who doubt"

Jude wrote, "Be merciful to those who doubt" (Jude 22). We are not to condemn those who struggle with doubts or look down on them; we should rather do all we can to support them. As we do so we should resist the temptation to speak too soon. Just as a doctor can only give the proper treatment once an accurate diagnosis has been made, so we will only be able to offer appropriate spiritual medicine to our friends once we have understood the nature and source of their doubts. We should listen before we speak. Listening in itself can be an encouragement to others as they begin to feel that someone else both cares and understands.

As we listen we should seek to discern what is at the root of a person's doubts. Two people might both say that they struggle to believe in God because of all the suffering in the world, but their doubts could have very different causes and should therefore be responded to in different ways. For one it may be a purely intellectual issue that demands a response that speaks to the mind. But for the other it may be a deeply emotional problem caused by personal suffering. If so, it is not appropriate to bombard such a vulnerable person with philosophical arguments.

After C. S. Lewis' wife died he wrote a diary in which he recorded his feelings. The day after adding one entry he commented, "I wrote that last night. It was a yell rather than a thought."[33] It was more a cry of pain from the heart than a rational expression from the mind. A wise Christian will recognize those times that call for sympathetic listening rather than theological discussion and respond accordingly.

The personality factor

As we have said, a wide variety of factors can trigger doubt, and each case requires a different approach. Certain personality types are especially prone to doubt. Some people are anxious by nature. They are the ones who are always worried as they drive away from the house that they might have left the iron on, even though they have already checked twice. Others are more naturally inclined to question authority, or to seek logical intellectual answers for every question. Still others have been so damaged by past hurts that they find it difficult to trust God's promises in the gospel. They are not to blame for their doubts, but they will need help to understand themselves and their doubts in the context of personality and circumstances.

Faith must be nurtured

We are responsible for some of the doubt we experience. It is hardly surprising that God feels distant and unreal if I am no longer making an effort to grow as a Christian.

> A living faith is a relationship, and like any relationship it must be cherished, nurtured, fostered and prized for itself . . . like an art or a skill, faith must not only be learned but kept in practice and developed. Just as a concert pianist practices for eight hours a day or a marathon runner covers twenty or thirty miles in road-training, so faith grows strong in believing but atrophies if out of use.[34]

As C. S. Lewis observed, "If you examined a hundred people who had lost their faith in Christianity, I wonder how many of them would turn out to have been reasoned out of it by honest argument? Do not most people simply drift away?"[35]

The drifting may start slowly but then, if not checked, quickly gathers pace. At first it may consist of infrequent times alone with God, irregular attendance at church after moving to a new area or small compromises with sin. As a result, God feels more distant than in the past and it is that much easier to take the next step down the path away from him. The further we go, the more distant he feels and the more likely it is that doubts will emerge.

At times the doubts can be both substantially caused by sin (because of the feeling of distance from God it can produce) and an excuse for it. One man had been a prayer partner of mine but, just a year later, he opposed me in a debate about the truth of Christianity. It was not that he had discovered some new objection to the faith. The problem was moral. He had begun a relationship with a non-Christian girl and so it became inconvenient for him to believe. There was little I could do to help him except urge him to repent.

Jesus once said, "If anyone chooses to do God's will, he will find out whether my teaching comes from God or whether I speak on my own" (Jn. 7:17). We should not be surprised if Jesus feels distant if we are turning from him and resisting his will for our lives. Some doubt is triggered chiefly by disobedience. In that case, the first step to recovery is to turn from our sin and "choose to do God's will" once more.

Wrong thinking

Some doubt is caused by wrong thinking. One writer observed:

> For some reason or other a believer gets into his head such a wrong idea of God that it comes between him and God or between him and his trusting God. Since he does not recognize what he is doing, he blames God rather than his faulty picture, little realizing that God is not like that at all. Unable to see God as he is, he cannot trust him as he should, and doubt is the result.[36]

The antidote for such doubt is right teaching about God from Scripture. We can point those who see God as a vindictive tyrant to the supreme picture of his self-sacrificial love on the cross. Others have received the impression that God is like a sugar daddy who will guarantee health and wealth to all his faithful people. When they resent him for not giving them what they want, they need to be reminded that God is concerned above all for our holiness rather than our short-term happiness. He is a loving Father who disciplines his children for our good (Heb. 12:7–11).

Responding to our own doubts

We cannot always help the thoughts that come into our hearts and the feelings that enter our heads, but we can make sure that we respond to them wisely. Rather than let doubt overwhelm us we should keep praying, maintain a right perspective and persevere in the Christian life.

Prayer

Never stop talking to God. He knows our thoughts and feelings, so there is no point hiding them from him. We could use the words of the man in the Gospels who said to Jesus: "I do believe; help me overcome my unbelief!" (Mk. 9:24).

Perspective

C. S. Lewis' *The Screwtape Letters* contains advice from a senior devil to a junior devil about how to torment Christians. In one letter he writes that the best way to make them atheists is to get them thinking, not about God, but about their own states of mind about God. As a result they will be so preoccupied by their own feelings and doubts that they stop turning to him.[37]

It is surprising how easily we are drawn into these thought patterns. One writer has observed, "Doubt is like an attention-seeking child: when you pay attention to it, it demands that you pay even more attention. You get locked into a vicious circle from which it is difficult to escape. If you feed doubts, they'll grow!"[38]

We should not ignore our doubts, but nor should we let them take over. In the midst of all the uncertainties we must keep reminding ourselves of what we can know. We should always maintain the right perspective and keep our focus on God.

Perseverance

Some people are perfectionists. They have over-tidy minds that cannot cope with loose ends. Their inclination is to put their Christian lives on hold until they have resolved all their questions. That is unrealistic, as we will always have some unresolved questions in this fallen world; but it is also unwise. Faith must be exercised or else it will weaken and even die. God calls us to persevere in the Christian life, despite our doubts, battling on until Christ returns and all our struggles end. On that day we will not just believe; we will see as well.

5

Depression

¹As the deer pants for streams of water,
*   so my soul pants for you, O God.*
²My soul thirsts for God, for the living God.
*   When can I go and meet with God?*
³My tears have been my food day and night,
while men say to me all day long,
*   "Where is your God?"*
⁴These things I remember as I pour out my soul:
how I used to go with the multitude,
leading the procession to the house of God,
with shouts of joy and thanksgiving among the festive
*   throng.*

⁵Why are you downcast, O my soul?
*   Why so disturbed within me?*
Put your hope in God,
*   for I will yet praise him,*
*   my Savior and ⁶my God.*

My soul is downcast within me;
*   therefore I will remember you*
from the land of the Jordan,
*   the heights of Hermon – from Mount Mizar.*

⁷Deep calls to deep
  in the roar of your waterfalls;
all your waves and breakers
  have swept over me.

⁸By day the LORD directs his love,
  at night his song is with me –
  a prayer to the God of my life.

⁹I say to God my Rock,
  "Why have you forgotten me?
Why must I go about mourning,
  oppressed by the enemy?"
¹⁰My bones suffer mortal agony
  as my foes taunt me,
saying to me all day long,
  "Where is your God?"

¹¹Why are you downcast, O my soul?
  Why so disturbed within me?
Put your hope in God,
  for I will yet praise him,
  my Savior and my God.

¹Vindicate me, O God,
  and plead my cause against an
  ungodly nation;
  rescue me from deceitful and wicked men.
²You are God my stronghold.
  Why have you rejected me?
Why must I go about mourning,
  oppressed by the enemy?
³Send forth your light and your truth, let them guide me;
  let them bring me to your holy mountain,
to the place where you dwell.

⁴Then will I go to the altar of God,
  to God, my joy and my delight.
I will praise you with the harp,
  O God, my God.

⁵Why are you downcast, O my soul?
  Why so disturbed within me?
Put your hope in God,
  for I will yet praise him,
  my Savior and my God.

Psalms 42 and 43

The Common Cold of the Mind

A young friend came to see me recently. I sensed that all was not well and asked him how he was doing. At first he put on a brave face and said he was fine but then the truth began to come out. He had been miserable for weeks. He did not know what was going on; he had never felt like this before. He had lost all his "get up and go" and had no enthusiasm for anything. His sleep was disturbed. Often he could not get to sleep in the first place; on other days he would wake up early in the morning, still exhausted, but incapable of getting back to sleep. It was always a struggle to drag himself out of bed; he wanted to stay there all day. He did not have any energy; everything was an effort. As a result he was beginning to get behind with his work and felt increasingly out of control. Everything was on top of him. He was frequently tearful; at times he could not stop crying. He knew he needed help but did not know where to turn. God seemed a million miles away and he felt isolated from his friends. They would not be able to understand what he was going through; he did not

understand it himself. He longed to be able to run away
and escape. At times he wished he had never been born;
in his worst moments he had contemplated suicide.
These disturbing thoughts added to a powerful sense of
guilt which was sometimes overwhelming. As a
Christian, should he not be full of joy? Surely these negative despairing feelings were symptoms of a deeply
sinful heart? But they were not. He was experiencing
some of the classic symptoms of a very common illness:
depression.

Depression has been described as "the common cold
of the mind" – not because it is only a minor complaint,
but because so many people suffer from it. It is estim-
ated that about a third of those who visit their doctor
are depressed to some degree. Anti-depressants are
among the most prescribed drugs. The word "depression" covers a broad range of experiences. We all feel
down sometimes. For some the periods occur more frequently and last longer, and the downs can be very low
indeed. There is no one cause. Depression can be due to
circumstances, past experiences, personality or simply
the body's chemistry. Christians are certainly not
immune. Far from preventing depression, our Christian
faith can even make the experience seem harder to deal
with. The illness affects every aspect of our lives and
personalities including our spirituality. Faith can add
another dimension to our suffering in the sense that, if
our feelings are deadened, we will no longer sense
God's presence as we used to. It can feel as if he has
abandoned us. That can lead in turn to the guilt my
friend described. In the words of the title of a helpful
Christian book on the subject, *I'm Not Supposed to Feel
Like This*.[39] Psalms 42 and 43 are helpful antidotes to that
way of thinking. The psalmist is a strong believer, but
he is also depressed.

Why are you downcast, O my soul?

Psalms 42 and 43 belong together. There is no heading at the beginning of Psalm 43. The two psalms form one poem in three sections, each ending with the same refrain:

> Why are you downcast, O my soul?
>> Why so disturbed within me?
> Put your hope in God, for I will yet praise him,
>> my Savior and my God.

Psalms 42:5, 11; 43:5

The psalmist is clearly very low. He feels spiritually dry; even deserted (v. 1). He is tearful and it seems he may also have lost his appetite (v. 3). He is "downcast" (we might say "flat") and "disturbed"; he has no peace within (v. 5). He is overwhelmed; everything is hanging over his head. He feels as if he is sinking (v. 7). And he is isolated, sensing that others are rejecting him (v. 9). It is a vivid and accurate description of depression.

Christians who face depression should be reassured that they are not alone. If the symptoms are persistent and significantly affect a person's daily life, he or she should see a doctor. Medication and "talking treatments," such as cognitive behavioral therapy, can make a real difference. It may also help to prescribe these psalms, to be taken with or without water, morning or evening – or perhaps both. Reading the Bible and praying are often a great struggle for those suffering from depression, so it is unrealistic to expect a deep meditation on every detail. Many have found it a great help just to read these words, which remind them that they are not alone. The psalmist has felt what they feel and his words give expression to their own experiences. They also recognize not just the voice of a fellow-sufferer, but also the word of God, speaking to them in their depression and helping them to respond to it in a godly way. I hope our study of these psalms will be an encouragement, not just to those who are struggling with depression, but to all of us as we face the ups and downs of life. They encourage us to both express and address our feelings.

1. Express Your Feelings

Our society's taboos concerning mental illness intensify the sense of isolation that those who suffer from depression experience. If we have the flu or break a leg, we think nothing about telling others; but if we are depressed, our instinct is to keep it to ourselves. We might feel ashamed and sense that others will look down on us if they know what we are going through. As a result, many people bottle up their feelings, scarcely even acknowledging them to themselves, let alone to others. There is no such escapism or embarrassment with the psalmist. He is open about how he feels: with himself and no doubt with others, even if only with a few trusted friends and with God. His example should spur us on to express our feelings rather than keep them hidden.

In each of the three sections of these psalms, the psalmist bares his soul. One commentator summarizes the psalmist's description of his mood in three words: "dry"; "drowning"; and "disheartened."[40]

Dry (Psalm 42:1–5)

> As the deer pants for streams of water,
> so my soul pants for you, O God.

> Psalm 42:1

An animal in a drought trudges wearily, desperately looking for water. Its tongue sticks to the roof of its mouth and it pants noisily. Here is a powerful depiction of a person who is desperate for God. Those who are depressed often suffer from low self-esteem. They may feel that everyone else is better and stronger – physically, mentally, spiritually. I know one Christian lady who suffered from severe depression, on and off, for many years. She once said to me, "I'm useless. My faith is so weak and I'm no good to anyone." That was certainly not how others in the church saw her. The way she battled on as a Christian despite her struggles was an inspiration to us. She had an amazing appetite for God. When she could not sense his presence with her, she did not give up; she cried out to him, like the psalmist did:

My soul thirsts for God, for the living God.
When can I go and meet with God?

Psalm 42:2

Far from being a sign of weak faith, those words express strong faith under considerable pressure. The psalmist does not give up. Despite the way he feels, he is determined to pursue God.

Others mocked him:

My tears have been my food day and night,
while men say to me all day long, "Where is your God?"

Psalm 42:3

No doubt he asked the same question as he heard their taunts: "Where are you, God?" Later in the psalm he asks, "Why have you forgotten me?" (42:9); "Why have you rejected me?" (43:2). But again, those cries are not

expressions of unbelief; they come from a heart of faith.
He longs to sense God's presence with him again.

Drowning (Psalm 42:6–11)

> My soul is downcast within me;
>   therefore I will remember you
> from the land of the Jordan,
>   the heights of Hermon – from Mount Mizar.
>
> Psalm 42:6

The title of the psalm tells us the writer was one of the
sons of Korah. The sons of Korah had special responsibility for leading music in the temple in Jerusalem. But
the psalmist is now a long way from the city in the north
of the country, near Mount Hermon. We are not told why
he is there,[41] but he is clearly miserable about it. He is
upset – not just because he is away from home, but also
because he feels cut off from God. He can no longer go to
worship God in the temple, which was the focal point of
God's presence for the people of Israel.

The psalmist describes the intensity of his feelings in
powerful imagery:

> Deep calls to deep
>   in the roar of your waterfalls;
> all your waves and breakers
>   have swept over me.
>
> Psalm 42:7

It is striking that he does not doubt that God is in control:
he speaks of "*your* waterfalls," "*your* waves and breakers." What he is experiencing is not simply bad luck; it is
all under God's sovereign control and direction. But that

thought brings confusion, not comfort. He says, in effect, "God, what are you doing? You're crushing me; you're overwhelming me and I can't take it." He feels like a pebble at the bottom of a waterfall, battered relentlessly by all that God throws at him. He is desperate for a stable place on which to stand, but as he cries out to God his rock, he hears no answer. It is as if he has been abandoned and left to cope on his own:

> I say to God my Rock,
>> "Why have you forgotten me?
> Why must I go about mourning,
>> oppressed by the enemy?"

Psalm 42:9

His feelings are so intense that they have a physical expression: "My bones suffer mortal agony" (v. 10). Depression does often affect the body, sometimes leading to aches and pains as well as more frequent illnesses.

Disheartened (Psalm 43:1–5)

> Vindicate me, O God,
>> and plead my cause against an
>> ungodly nation;
> rescue me from deceitful
>> and wicked men.

Psalm 43:1

Surrounded by ungodly people who oppose him and cannot be trusted, the psalmist cries out to God but hears no reply. In his desperation, with nowhere else to turn, he runs to God for protection, but he feels as if his cries for help are ignored:

You are God my stronghold.
  Why have you rejected me?
Why must I go about mourning,
  oppressed by the enemy?

Psalm 43:2

C. S. Lewis describes his experiences after the death of his
wife in a starkly honest book, *A Grief Observed*. He writes:

> Meanwhile, where is God? Go to him when your need is
> desperate, when all other help is in vain, and what do you
> find? A door slammed in your face, and a sound of bolting
> and double bolting on the inside. After that, silence.[42]

God does not abandon his people, but that is sometimes
what it feels like. Even the most faithful believers can
experience deep depression and a sense of spiritual des-
olation. Charles Spurgeon, who suffered from frequent
bouts of depression, once said: "There are dungeons
beneath the Castle of Despair."[43] We should not be surprised if this is an experience we have to undergo. It is
not a sign that our faith is weak nor is it something to be
ashamed of and kept to ourselves. The example of the
psalmist is an encouragement to express our feelings. We
might not want the whole world to know but, at the very
least, we should talk to one or two trusted friends. And
we should talk to God and tell him how we feel. He
knows anyway, so there is no point in pretending. He
understands us perfectly and loves us deeply.

2. Address Your Feelings

Why are you downcast, O my soul?
  Why so disturbed within me?

Put your hope in God,
  for I will yet praise him,
  my Savior and my God.

Psalms 42:5; 11; 43:5

We are not simply to express our feelings, we should also address them. That is what the psalmist is doing in the refrain of these psalms (42:5, 11; 43:5). It is often said that talking to yourself is the first sign of mental illness, but it may also be the first step to recovery in times of depression. In a helpful article on depression one writer, reflecting on his own experience, warns: "Your mind will tell you things that are not true."[44] Negative emotions and thinking are features of depression. We can convince ourselves: "It's all my fault"; "No one loves me"; "I'll never feel better again"; "There's no hope"; "God has rejected me." But our feelings often reflect distortions of the truth or even lies. Instead of accepting them, we need to learn to talk back. That is the advice of Martyn Lloyd-Jones in the first chapter of his book, *Spiritual Depression*:

> Have you realised that most of your unhappiness is due to the fact that you are listening to yourself instead of talking to yourself? Take those thoughts that come to you the moment you wake up in the morning. You have not originated them but they start talking to you, they bring back the problems of yesterday . . . Somebody is talking. Who is talking to you? Yourself is talking to you . . . The essence of the matter is to understand that this self of ours, this other man within us, has got to be handled. Do not listen to him; turn on him; encourage him; remind him of what you know, instead of listening placidly to him and allowing him to drag you down and depress you. For that is what he will always do if you allow him to be in control.[45]

Having expressed our feelings, we must not let them control us. We need to learn, as it were, to take ourselves in hand: to talk to ourselves, question ourselves and exhort ourselves. The psalmist is a good example to follow.

Look in

> Why are you downcast, O my soul?
>   Why so disturbed within me?
>
> Psalms 42:5a, 11a; 43:5a

The psalmist looks within himself and asks the question "why?" He tries to understand the cause of his despair. That is a good place to start if we are feeling low: "Why do I feel like this?"

There may be a perfectly logical reason for why we feel as we do. Sometimes we have to undergo difficult circumstances. We should expect that a bereavement or illness will affect our mood. But sometimes, once we examine the cause of our distress, we can see that it is based on a misunderstanding or an over-reaction. John Piper has written a brief biographical account of William Cowper, the eighteenth-century poet who was a fervent believer in Christ and long-term sufferer from depression. Piper draws this lesson from his life: "We fortify ourselves against the dark hours of depression by cultivating a deep distrust of the certainties of despair."[46] It is helpful to look within and ask ourselves: "Are things really as bad as they seem?" If the answer is yes, we can ask further questions: "Is there really no silver lining in the cloud or light in the darkness? Is there nothing to be thankful for in the midst of the gloom?"

We should be cautious when we ask such questions of others. Any approach to a depressed person which they could interpret as a version of, "Come on, cheer up and pull yourself together; it's not that bad," could just discourage them further. But what may not be helpful coming from others can be very helpful when we apply it ourselves. It is good to ask that question "why?": "Why are you downcast, O my soul?"

Look back

> These things I remember
>   as I pour out my soul:
> how I used to go with the multitude,
>   leading the procession to the house of God,
> with shouts of joy and thanksgiving
>   among the festive throng.
>
>   Psalm 42:4

The psalmist also looks back as he speaks to himself and addresses his feelings. He remembers good times in the past, in this case the great festivals of the Jewish calendar when crowds would converge on Jerusalem and head in procession to the temple. As one of the sons of Korah, he would have had an important role in leading the music. They were times of great joy when God felt real and close.

It is possible for such recollections of past joy to make things worse. J. B. Phillips, the Bible translator, had a severe mental breakdown. When asked to describe how he felt, one of the aspects of his depression that he identified was what he called "agony by comparison."[47] He found it almost unbearable to remember good times in the past because those memories only reminded him how miserable he was by contrast in the present. But recalling spiritual highpoints in our lives can also be helpful. It may be that God feels very distant now. If so, it can help to remember that that has not always been the case. We could think, perhaps, of those early days after conversion when we were on a spiritual high for days, or of times of blessing when God was clearly at work in us and through us.

In the New International Version, Psalm 42:8 appears to speak of such a time of spiritual blessedness: "By day the LORD directs his love, at night his song is with me – a prayer to the God of my life." Those words might seem out of place sandwiched between the gloom of verses 7 and 9, but our spiritual experience can be like that. We can suffer great lows and then find relief, when all seems well again. But that is not necessarily the end of the depression; it can quickly return.

However, verse 8 could also be translated: "By day the LORD used to direct his love, at night his song used to be with me" (the verbs are in the imperfect tense). It may be that, as in verse 4, the psalmist is recalling past times of spiritual exhilaration when God seemed very real. Such memories can be an encouragement to persevere in faith, even in the darkest times. What we have enjoyed in the past could be our experience again in this life and will certainly be far surpassed in heaven, so it is worth pressing on.

Look forward

> Put your hope in God,
>   for I will yet praise him,
>   my Savior and my God.

Psalms 42:5b, 11b; 43:5b

Those words express a determination in the present: "I *will* keep praising God, even when I have to do it through gritted teeth." "I will keep going to church, meeting with God's people and singing his praises, even when it's the last thing I feel like doing." But the writer expresses more than that. He speaks not simply of a resolve in the present, but also of a conviction for the future. He is sure that one day the dark cloud will lift and he will sense again the light of God's presence and be full of praise. It seems that that hope grows in him as we progress through these two psalms. The depression is still there right to the end (43:5), but he is confident that it will pass one day:

> Send forth your light and your truth,
>   let them guide me;
> let them bring me to your holy mountain,
>   to the place where you dwell.
> Then will I go to the altar of God,
>   to God, my joy and my delight.
> I will praise you with the harp,
>   O God, my God.

Psalm 43:3–4

If the psalmist could look to the future with hope surely we today, who live after the coming of Christ, have even more reason to do so. We are bound to think of Christ when we read this psalm. It is likely Christ was alluding to it when he cried out in the garden of Gethsemane: "My soul is overwhelmed with sorrow" (Mk. 14:34); "My heart is troubled" (Jn. 12:27). He was thirsty as he hung on the cross and felt submerged, overwhelmed by the waters of judgement. He did not just feel forsaken by God his Father – he really was forsaken, as he faced the penalty for human sin. We worship the Messiah who knows what it is like to suffer, and his suffering far out-weighed even the agony of a deep depression. Yet he put his hope in God and was vindicated. God raised him from the dead and seated him at his right hand in heaven. Because he died and rose again, all who trust in him can face the future with great hope, no matter how difficult our present circumstances may be. Our tears may be our food day and night, but the day is coming when Christ will wipe away every tear. We may go about mourning, oppressed by the enemy, but the day is coming when there will be "no more death or mourning or crying or pain" (Rev. 21:4). And there will be no more enemies; even the great enemy, the devil, will be banished. Then we will enjoy life forever in God's perfect new creation. Nothing will spoil it: neither physical ailments nor mental anguish. Then, at last, all the deep longings of our hearts will be fulfilled. We will no longer be panting or thirsting for God. We will see him face to face and will have eternity to drink our fill from the river of life.

Meanwhile, we may well have to suffer greatly. God does not promise an easy ride for the Christian. It may be that we have to endure dark days of depression. If so, we should let these psalms encourage and challenge us. We are to express our feelings, at least to God and a few trusted friends, rather than bottle them up. And we should address our feelings: looking in, looking back and looking forward:

> Why are you downcast, O my soul?
> 　Why so disturbed within me?
> Put your hope in God,
> 　for I will yet praise him,
> 　my Savior and my God.

Psalms 42:5, 11; 43:5

6

Pride

³³*They came to Capernaum. When he was in the house, he asked them, "What were you arguing about on the road?"* ³⁴*But they kept quiet because on the way they had argued about who was the greatest.*

³⁵*Sitting down, Jesus called the Twelve and said, "If anyone wants to be first, he must be the very last, and the servant of all."*

³⁶*He took a little child and had him stand among them. Taking him in his arms, he said to them,* ³⁷*"Whoever welcomes one of these little children in my name welcomes me; and whoever welcomes me does not welcome me but the one who sent me."*

³⁸*"Teacher," said John, "we saw a man driving out demons in your name and we told him to stop, because he was not one of us."*

³⁹*"Do not stop him," Jesus said. "No one who does a miracle in my name can in the next moment say anything bad about me,* ⁴⁰*for whoever is not against us is for us.* ⁴¹*I tell you the truth, anyone who gives you a cup of water in my name because you belong to Christ will certainly not lose his reward.*

Mark 9:33–41

"The Great Sin"

What do you think is the worst sin? An action like murder or rape? Or perhaps an attitude such as selfishness, lust or greed? C. S. Lewis, in his book *Mere Christianity*, called one chapter "The Great Sin." He writes:

> There is one vice of which no man in the world is free; which everyone else in the world knows when he sees it in someone else; and of which hardly any people . . . ever imagine that they are guilty of themselves . . . The essential vice, the utmost evil is pride. Unchastity, anger, greed, drunkenness and all that, are mere fleabites in comparison; it was through pride that the devil became the devil; pride leads to every other vice; it is the complete anti-God state of mind.[48]

If that sounds like overstatement we need to consider the nature of pride. It is, essentially, an over-inflated ego: the attitude that places me at the centre of everything. It is what causes me to bristle when someone cuts me up when I am driving, fails to acknowledge me at a party or patronizes me in some way: "How dare they do that to *me*!" We hate others treating us as if we are beneath them because we like to think we are above them. Our pride loves to see our name in lights, to score all the goals or get all the praise for a successful job at work.

Pride is so serious because it does not just clash with other people; it clashes with God. It says, "I am at the centre of everything" when, in fact, God is at the centre. Before I can come to know him and be accepted by him I have to be willing to acknowledge reality and admit that he is far greater than me and that I am nothing compared to him. That admission does not come naturally to me, and so my pride cuts me off from God. Proud people are always looking down on others and, as long as we look down, we are unable to see the great God who is infinitely above us. So pride is the very essence of sin. It is what leads me to refuse to submit to God and to go my own way in the first place. That rejection of God's authority then leads in turn to all other sins I commit. C. S. Lewis was right to call it "the great sin."

"The first sin"

According to Jonathan Edwards, the eighteenth-century New England Puritan, pride is not only the great sin, but also the first. He writes, "Pride is the worst viper that is in the heart, the great disturber of the soul's peace and sweet communion with Christ; it was the first sin that ever was."[49]

Satan offered the forbidden fruit to Adam and Eve in the garden and promised that if they ate of it they would "be like God, knowing good and evil" (Gen. 3:5). That thought was very attractive to them. Why should they be content to stay beneath God, taking orders from him? They loved the idea of being able to strut around as gods themselves within the garden, rather than submitting to their Creator. So, in their pride, they took the fruit in a bid to exalt themselves. The sad irony, of course, is that they suffered a terrible fall: from the dignity of being holy people, perfectly reflecting God's image, to the dehumanizing depravity of sin. We have all followed in their proud footsteps ever since.

The way of the cross

Many years after the first Adam, a second Adam came. The Lord Jesus Christ, the perfect human being, shows us another way to live. He said, "even the Son of Man did not come to be served, but to serve, and to give his life as a ransom for many" (Mk. 10:45). Although he is God, high above all, he lowered himself so that he might lift us up and restore us to a right relationship with his Father.

It took a long time for the disciples to recognize who Jesus is. When at last Peter made his confession, "You are the Christ" (Mk. 8:29), Mark tells us, "He [Jesus] then began to teach them that the Son of Man must suffer many things and be rejected by the elders, chief priests and teachers of the law, and that he must be killed and after three days rise again" (Mk. 8:31). This is the turning point of Mark's Gospel. After that, Jesus headed to Jerusalem to accomplish his task as the suffering servant, to die in the place of his people. As he traveled, he taught his disciples that his example of humble service was to be the pattern for their lives. They were to prepare to follow him in the way of the cross: "If anyone would come after me, he must deny himself and take up his cross and follow me" (Mk. 8:34).

Pride was so deeply rooted in the disciples' hearts that they failed to understand and accept Jesus' message. Jesus once again foretold his death: "The Son of Man is going to be betrayed into the hands of men. They will kill him, and after three days he will rise" (Mk. 9:31). Mark tells us, "But they did not understand what he meant and were afraid to ask him about it" (Mk. 9:32). The passage that follows, which we are thinking about in this chapter, makes it very clear that they did not understand. The Lord Jesus taught three lessons that challenged the disciples' pride and continue to challenge us today.

1. Don't let pride distort your view of yourself (vv. 33–35)

2. Don't let pride distort your treatment of others (vv. 36–37)

3. Don't let pride distort your opinion of others (vv. 38–41)

1. Don't Let Pride Distort Your View of Yourself (Mark 9:33–35)

Who is the greatest?

The disciples were relaxing after a hard day's journey when Jesus asked them, "What were you arguing about on the road?" There was an awkward silence. No one wanted to admit that they were having a childish argument about which of them was the greatest. It is not surprising that they were embarrassed. Jesus had just told them that he would give up his life for them but his humble example did not dent their pride; they were still only interested in exalting themselves. Many of us can identify with that ambition. We want to rise above others in academic results, at work, or in a club or society. We can also seek to gain credit through the successes of our children or grandchildren.

A topsy-turvy kingdom

It is striking that Jesus does not rebuke the disciples for their discussion. Instead he says, in effect, "All right, if you want to be great, let me tell you how to achieve it." His advice is not what they were expecting: "If anyone wants to be first, he must be the very last, and the servant of all" (v. 35). Everything is topsy-turvy in the kingdom of God. If we want to be great, we must be willing to be small; if we wish to be first, we must be last. The great one is not the king, the emperor or the bishop. The great one is the servant. The way to greatness in God's eyes is the path of humble, sacrificial service. Jesus is the supreme example of that truth. He now sits enthroned at the right hand of his Father in heaven in the position of ultimate authority in the universe, but he had to stoop very low before his coronation.

> He humbled himself
> and became obedient to death –
> even death on a cross!
> Therefore God exalted him to the highest place
> and gave him the name that is above every name,
> that at the name of Jesus every knee should bow,
> in heaven and on earth and under the earth,
> and every tongue confess that Jesus Christ is Lord,
> to the glory of God the Father.
>
> Philippians 2:8–11

"A most superior person"

Some of us think we are rather special. We may not boast to others, but inwardly we glow with self-satisfaction. We would not call ourselves "great," that would be going too far; but we are pleased with ourselves. We have managed to rise above most of those around us. As long as I can think of some who are beneath me, I feel good about myself. "I am at a top university or do an impressive job. I have staff under me. I have the kind of home and car that people envy. I am a respected leader in my church and social group. I am significant."

George Curzon was one of the brightest of his generation at Oxford University, where he was President of the Union. He became viceroy of India at the age of thirty-nine, ruling a nation of millions, before finishing his political career as Foreign Secretary. He was a brilliant man and he knew it. A contemporary commented that his manner in parliament was that of "a divinity addressing black beetles." He was mocked in the words of a ditty: "My name is George Nathaniel Curzon, a most superior person." There are some people like that who exude an air of superiority. Their pride is obvious.

Perhaps you see nothing of yourself in a man like Curzon. You are a quiet, understated person who prefers to stay in the background. You have little time for those pushy people who are always striving to achieve things. You rather despise those who have their noses in the air and act as if they are so important. But, in looking down on them, are you not guilty of the very pride of which you accuse them? It is even possible to pride ourselves on our humility, like the imaginary author of an autobiography entitled, "Humility and How I Achieved It."

However our pride manifests itself, Jesus challenges us not to allow it to distort our view of ourselves. True greatness is found in following the footsteps of Jesus: "If anyone wants to be first, he must be the very last, and the servant of all" (v. 35).

2. Don't Let Pride Distort Your Treatment of Others (Mark 9:36–37)

A visual aid

Having taught that greatness in the kingdom of God demands humble service, Jesus now tells us in verses 36 and 37 what that will mean in practice. He uses a visual aid to make his point. He takes a little child in his arms and says "Whoever welcomes one of these little children in my name welcomes me; and whoever welcomes me does not welcome me but the one who sent me" (v. 37).

While a boy recently took his father to the European Court for beating him, nothing like that could have happened in first-century Palestine. Children had no rights or status in society at all. So Jesus is saying, "If you are to be a servant, you must be prepared to welcome people like this – the unimpressive people who everyone else ignores; the lowest of the low."

In our pride we often do not bother with those we consider beneath us; we sometimes subconsciously decide that they are not worth our time or attention. If we do smile at them and say hello, we feel good about ourselves and think we have done our bit, but we do not make time for anything more. We have more important people to speak to. Besides, we do not want to get too friendly with those who do not quite belong to our crowd. After all, if we are seen talking too long to that unpopular man in the next office or to that girl down the street, others might think we are their friends and that would not do our image any good. So, at most, we will be friendly when no one else is looking but, for the rest of the time, we will keep our distance. But our attitude towards those who have a high status, the powerful and popular, is very different. We go out of our way to be friendly to them and hope that others notice; it might do us good to be associated with them.

Our pride distorts how we see others and how we act towards them. It prompts us to be interested only in the great and the good. But Jesus turns the standards of this world upside down. As his followers, citizens of the kingdom of God, we are called to live a very different way. We are to suppress our pride and humbly serve those whom others would regard as beneath us.

A perfect model

Jesus provides us with the perfect model to follow. The respectable people in Israel were horrified that he spent so much time with "tax collectors and 'sinners,'" the dregs of society who they took pains to avoid (Mk. 2:15–17). He showed love and compassion to those who were shunned and despised by others: the hated Samaritans (Lk. 17:16; Jn. 4:9), unclean lepers (Mk. 1:40–41), an adulterous woman (Jn. 8:11) and an enemy soldier (Lk. 7:1–10). His life of humble service reached its climax at the cross, where he gave up his life for sinners like us. He was willing to die so that he might welcome us as his friends. His relationship with us certainly does not enhance his status. We are infinitely lower than he is, and yet he stoops to lift us up. In the world's eyes, this is sheer folly. The world cannot understand why God should choose to be associated with "the lowly things of this world and the despised things – and the things that are not" (1 Cor. 1:28). But God calls on us to live the same way: to ignore the hierarchies and class systems of the world and show love to all, regardless of their social rank.

I was very struck by the Christian group at my school when I was first converted. In the rest of school life there was a clearly defined social structure. Everyone knew their place. Senior boys would only talk to the juniors to tell them off. But at the Christian meeting I noticed some of my fellow senior students warmly welcoming boys from the first year. They remembered their names, got them a cup of coffee and asked how they were doing. These "gods" of the school, prefects and sports captains, were relating quite naturally to the new boys who the rest of their classmates regarded with contempt. They were following the example of Christ.

Loving the unloved

If I am to obey Christ's teaching in Mark 9:37 I must ask myself, "Who are those with little status in the particular world I inhabit?" They are the ones to whom I must be welcoming and open hearted. I should be willing to serve them.

In every community there are individuals who are rejected by the majority. At school they may be the victims of physical or psychological violence. Adults often have more subtle means of bullying, but they are equally effective in destroying the lives of those who do not fit in. Some people suffer not from being victimized, but just because they are ignored. Most employees have little or no time for those of the lowest rank at work: the car park attendant, cleaner or work experience student. But Christians are called to be different.

A friend of mine once worked as a maid in a hotel. She remained invisible to most guests; it was as if she did not exist. Others treated her like dirt, issuing orders and complaints with never a word of thanks. Sadly she noticed little difference when a Christian group came to stay, although all of her fellow staff did notice the conduct of one man, a distinguished Christian preacher. He showed an interest in everyone and was unfailingly courteous, kind and grateful. In my friend's experience, such conduct was very rare.

In many cultures the elderly are treated with special respect, but the opposite is increasingly the case in the Western world. Our youthful, frenetic society has little time for those who cannot keep up with the pace. They are too often left on their own in a lonely house or institution: out of sight and out of mind. There are increasing demands for legislation to allow for voluntary euthanasia. If such evil was sanctioned, there would undoubtedly be those who would feel it was their duty to die so that they would no longer be a burden to others. It may at first appear that we do not have much to gain from caring for the elderly. Contact with them may not boost our status in the eyes of others, even if there are other rewards, but it is people like them that Jesus calls his followers to serve.

We may speak strongly against racism, but it remains as a sinful instinct in our hearts. Speaking as a Briton, I can say that we tend to treat people from other cultures appallingly. We may not mean to be unfriendly or rude. It could be a natural reserve that holds us back, but we still give the impression that we are aloof and lacking in warmth. Many nations greet asylum seekers with tabloid hostility and local suspicion. Where are the Christians who will befriend them, teach them English and offer them hospitality? Many overseas students spend years in our universities without ever seeing the inside of a national's home. Even when they make the effort to come to our churches, they are frequently ignored. We hold back from engaging with them, worried that we may not be able to understand what they say or will have little in common with them, without thinking of the awkwardness they must always feel as outsiders in our culture.

In Britain, the numbers attending churches have rapidly declined across all social groups over the last few decades, but the greatest decline has been among poorer communities. Most thriving evangelical churches are in middle-class areas. Attempts have been made in recent years to formulate a strategy to reach the poor with the good news of Christ. That is an important task, but any new outreach must focus first not on strategy, but on attitude. Are we only interested in those we think can help us in some way, whether materially or socially? Or are we prepared, like Christ, to serve those from whom, in the world's eyes, we will gain nothing?

"In Christ's name"

The church should be a counter-culture which refuses to operate according to the social divisions of our society. We should welcome people of all races, personalities, cultures and backgrounds. Above all we should not regard them as black or white, rich or poor, native or foreign, but as those for whom Christ died – and we should treat them accordingly. If we do so, our acts of humble service will not be without significance. Jesus says, "Whoever welcomes one of these little children in my name welcomes me; and whoever welcomes me does not welcome me but the one who sent me" (Mk. 9:37).

Jesus is not teaching that anyone who is kind to children, or others of low social status, is automatically saved. Nor is he making a comment on the spiritual state of children. We should notice that he is referring to welcoming that is done "in my name." He speaks of outreach that is done for him by those who believe in him and seek to serve him. Our pride tells us we should not bother even to notice those who are beneath us; but Jesus tells us that it could not be more important. When we do something *for* Jesus, we are doing it *to* him. That quick visit to a lonely person at the end of a busy day may seem insignificant, but we should in fact see it as a visit to Jesus. More than that, it is a visit to our heavenly Father. And when, in obedience to Christ, we go out of our way to befriend an outsider in our community, we are welcoming not just a fellow human being, but our Lord and his Father as well. Jesus challenges us not to let pride distort our treatment of others, but rather to follow his example of humble service to all.

3. Don't Let Pride Distort Your Opinion of Others (Mark 9:38–41)

"Not one of us"

John approached Jesus and said, "Teacher, we saw a man driving out demons in your name and we told him to stop, because he was not one of us" (v. 38). Those last six words are the significant ones. What upset John was that this man did not belong to the small inner circle of Jesus' disciples.

By this time in the Gospels the twelve disciples had begun to understand that they were special. They had been set apart by Jesus to live closely with him and to receive extra teaching and training. They must have felt good about that: they were right at the heart of Jesus' mission. But then they heard about another man who was driving out demons in Jesus' name and they felt threatened because he was not one of their inner circle. If anyone other than Jesus was going to perform miracles, surely it should be one of them. It was all most irregular; the man had to be stopped!

No doubt their arrogance was heightened by the fact that, only days before, they had been unable to drive out an evil spirit themselves. While Jesus had been up a mountain with Peter, James and John, a man had brought his demon-possessed son to the other disciples, but they had not been able to help. When Jesus later arrived the father told him, "I asked your disciples to drive out the spirit, but they could not" (Mk. 9:18). They must have smarted at Jesus' reply: "O unbelieving generation, how long shall I stay with you? How long shall I put up with you? Bring the boy to me" (Mk. 9:19). Jesus then cast the spirit out of the boy.

"Whoever is not against us is for us"

Pride is certainly behind the disciples' negative reaction to the man who is driving out demons and Jesus rebukes them for it: "Do not stop him. No one who does a miracle in my name can in the next moment say anything bad about me, for whoever is not against us is for us" (vv. 39–40).

Taken out of context, Jesus' words, "whoever is not against us is for us," could be understood to mean that we should accept everyone as Christians unless they are actively opposed to him. But it is clear from the context that he is not teaching that. In verse 39 he points out the stupidity of John's negative reaction to the man. How could he be regarded as an enemy of Christ who should be opposed if he has just performed a miracle in Christ's name?

To do something "in the name of Christ" means more than using it as a magic formula. That would never work, as the sons of Sceva in Ephesus found out. They did not know Christ and yet they tried to cast out an evil spirit using his name. The spirit answered them: "Jesus I know, and I know about Paul, but who are you?" Luke tells us: "Then the man who had the evil spirit jumped on them and overpowered them all. He gave them such a beating that they ran out of the house naked and bleeding" (Acts 19:15–16). The man in Mark 9 would have been equally unsuccessful if he had evoked Christ's name in a similar way without having faith in him. But the fact that he was able to drive out demons demonstrated that he was a Christian with a real faith. Christ had been at work through him. Having proved that he was "for" Christ, he was hardly likely to speak "against" him. He should be regarded therefore as a friend, not an enemy.

Jesus tells us more about who he means by "those who are not against us" in verse 41: "I tell you the truth, anyone who gives you a cup of water in my name because you belong to Christ will certainly not lose his reward."

Jesus is instructing his disciples that they should accept any true follower of his. Such followers do not have to cast out demons or perform other miracles to prove their authenticity. They are revealed also by their conduct towards Christians. If, for example, someone takes pity on the disciples as they travel in Christ's service and gives them a drink of water, that person will not go unrewarded. He or she has not simply performed a random act of kindness. We are told it is done "in his name," which means it is prompted by faith in Christ. The individual reveals himself to be a true disciple through his love for Christian brothers and will therefore receive a disciple's reward; he is a friend of God. Jesus' point is clear: if God accepts a person, so should the apostles.

Be discerning, but positive

We should not stretch this teaching too far. Jesus' words do not contradict what he says elsewhere about the need to be discerning. He warns us to "Watch out for false prophets. They come to you in sheep's clothing, but inwardly they are ferocious wolves" (Mtt. 7:15). Not all who claim to speak, or even perform miracles, in the name of Christ truly belong to him. Fellowship cannot be indiscriminate. There are times when it is right to break communion with those who claim to be Christians because of their false teaching or unrepentant sinful acts (1 Cor. 5:1–5; Titus 1:10–11; Rev. 2:20).

While we should not stretch the application of Jesus' teaching in Mark 9:38–41, it is also important that we do not ignore its challenge. Like the disciples, we are quick to allow pride to distort our opinions of others. We find it hard to accept that those who are "not one of us," but belong to a different Christian group, could really be responsible for any spiritual good.

A few years ago when I was working in Johannesburg, I was troubled when a student I had discipled spoke to me about another church in the area. I had some theological disagreements with the leadership of this particular church, but there was no doubt that they were genuine Christians. What upset me most was not so much that the young man spoke so dismissively about the church, but that he clearly thought I would be delighted that he did so. He was copying the example I had unconsciously been giving him. I felt like Dr. Frankenstein must have felt after creating his monster and I thought to myself, "What have I done? It's my fault that he is so critical of others." Seeing my own harsh attitude reflected in someone else made me realize how ugly it was and that I needed to repent.

Of course we should be discerning. It will be right at times to recognize the errors of others. But we should never forget that, if they belong to Christ, they are our brothers and sisters and we should treat them accordingly. If at times we have to disagree with them, we must do so with gentleness and respect, and never with relish or from party spirit. When we are noticing their faults, we should also take pains to appreciate their virtues.

In our pride we often fail to recognize anything good in those who do not belong to our particular group. If we hear reports of conversions in another church we think to ourselves, "They're probably not genuine – I doubt they'll last." When we listen to a speaker from a different Christian background our spiritual antennae are twitching as we look for errors. If we search hard enough, we will probably find something to complain about, and that is what will remain in our hearts and minds. So we comment to a friend afterwards, "I wasn't at all convinced by his understanding of verse 29," but we forget entirely all the good teaching he drew from verses 1–28.

"He will be so near the throne"

John Wesley and George Whitefield were the two great English evangelical leaders of the eighteenth century. Both were used mightily as evangelists and were the major human agents of the revival that swept the country. Although they had worked closely together in the early days, they then drifted apart because of theological differences. At times the division was sharp, especially among their followers. One of Whitefield's men asked him one day if they would see Wesley in heaven. Whitefield began his reply in a way that no doubt confirmed the suspicions of his supporters: "I fear not." But then he continued, "He will be so near the eternal throne and we at such a distance we shall hardly get a sight of him."[50] We should do all we can to exhibit a similarly humble attitude towards other genuine believers, even if we differ from them on secondary matters. We would do well to examine ourselves and ask in every situation, "How much in my negative reaction to that other Christian or group is a result of genuine concern for truth, and how much is a result of pride?" We must not let pride distort our opinion of others.

"He died for me"

There is a story that, after the American Civil War, a man was seen kneeling at a soldier's grave near Nashville. A passerby asked him if his son was buried there. "No," he replied, "My family was sick when I was called up to fight and they depended on me. A friend, who was unmarried, volunteered to take my place. He was wounded at Chickamauga and was carried to the hospital here, where he died. I have traveled many miles so I can write on his grave, 'He died for me.'"

All Christians can say the same of Jesus Christ. Although he is the King of Kings and Lord of Lords, he willingly left the glory of heaven so that he could give up his life for us. His humble example rebukes us for our pride and challenges us to repent.

C. S. Lewis was right to call pride "the great sin." It corrupts our relationship with God and with other people. As we recognize this poison in our hearts we should apply the only antidote: the cross of Christ. The cross not only provides a means of forgiveness for all sin, even our pride, it also presents a model of a different way to live: the path of humble service.

When I survey the wondrous cross
On which the Prince of glory died,
My richest gain I count but loss,
And pour contempt on all my pride.[51]

7

Homosexuality

Some Pharisees came to him to test him. They asked, "Is it lawful for a man to divorce his wife for any and every reason?"

⁴"Haven't you read," he replied, "that at the beginning the Creator 'made them male and female,' ⁵and said, 'For this reason a man will leave his father and mother and be united to his wife, and the two will become one flesh'? ⁶So they are no longer two, but one. Therefore what God has joined together, let man not separate."

⁷"Why then," they asked, "did Moses command that a man give his wife a certificate of divorce and send her away?"

⁸Jesus replied, "Moses permitted you to divorce your wives because your hearts were hard. But it was not this way from the beginning. ⁹I tell you that anyone who divorces his wife, except for marital unfaithfulness, and marries another woman commits adultery."

¹⁰The disciples said to him, "If this is the situation between a husband and wife, it is better not to marry."

¹¹Jesus replied, "Not everyone can accept this word, but only those to whom it has been given. ¹²For some are eunuchs because they were born that way; others were made that way by men; and others have renounced marriage because of the kingdom of heaven. The one who can accept this should accept it."

Matthew 19:3–12

⁹Do you not know that the wicked will not inherit the kingdom of God? Do not be deceived: Neither the sexually immoral nor idolaters nor adulterers nor male prostitutes nor homosexual offenders ¹⁰nor thieves nor the greedy nor drunkards nor slanderers nor swindlers will inherit the kingdom of God. ¹¹And that is what some of you were. But you were washed, you were sanctified, you were justified in the name of the Lord Jesus Christ and by the Spirit of our God.

1 Corinthians 6:9–11

A whirlwind of change

The last few decades have seen rapid changes in attitudes to homosexuality. It was only in 1967 that homosexual acts between consenting adult males were made legal in Britain. Homosexuality was officially considered to be a form of mental illness by the American Psychiatric Association until 1973. Since then we have witnessed a whirlwind of change. It is now commonly believed that homosexual practice is not immoral or deviant but is entirely natural for some. So to have a different age of consent for homosexual acts, to deny homosexual partners the right to adopt, or to give heterosexual marriage a distinct status in the eyes of the law which is not afforded to committed homosexual partnerships, is seen by many as a breach of human rights equivalent to discrimination on the basis of race, gender, or disability.

The changes in society have led to deep divisions in the church. Liberal revisionist Christians in the West have argued for a change to the traditional Christian understanding that the only right context for sex is within heterosexual marriage. They have been resisted by orthodox Christians who rightly believe that the issues at stake go deeper than the issue of homosexuality alone but concern our understanding of scripture, sin and salvation. There is a danger in all these debates and disagreements, however necessary they may be, that we forget that homosexuality is not simply an "issue"; it concerns people, created and loved by God, many of whom are Christians. In this chapter I am not attempting to address the controversies concerning homosexuality in society and the church, but am rather writing to those individuals for whom this is a very personal subject.[2]

Statistics

We can not be sure how many people feel same-sex attraction. The Kinsey Report of 1948[52] concluded that 4% of white American men are exclusively homosexual throughout their lives and 10% for up to three years. These figures are still widely quoted, although Kinsey's research methods have now been discredited. The most extensive recent surveys of sexual experience in Britain and America indicate that 6.1% (UK) and 9.1% (USA) of men and 3.4% (UK) and 4.3% (USA) of women have had some kind of sexual experience with someone of the same sex. A significant number of the men had this experience before the age of 18 and never repeated it. Only 3.6% (UK) and 4.1% (USA) of men and 1.7% (UK) and 2.2% (USA) of women admit to genital contact with someone of the same sex in the previous five years.[53]

We should be wary of drawing any firm conclusions from these figures. Human sexuality is more complicated than is commonly imagined and is perhaps best seen as making up a complex spectrum. While some are at either end (only ever being attracted to the opposite – or their own – sex), others are nearer the middle. Our place on that spectrum may well not be fixed. Many who knew same-sex attraction in their youth have never experienced it again in later life; others are surprised by the sudden emergence of such attraction in middle age. Having quoted various surveys in the Western world one writer concludes that perhaps "less than 2% of the male population and less than 1% of the female, are exclusively homosexual in inclination and practice".[3] However, a considerably larger proportion of people has experienced same-sex attraction at some time and may have wondered as a result whether they are homosexual, even if they have never acted on their feelings. We can be sure that there is a significant number in a typical congregation for whom homosexuality is not simply a political issue in society or the church but is a deeply personal one.

Causes

There is no clear consensus as to why people experience same-sex sexual attraction. Some argue for a predominantly biological cause. A few studies have been widely quoted as supporting an association between homosexual behaviour and certain hormones or genes, but these have been widely disputed and have not been generally accepted in the scientific community.

Other theories focus on environmental factors. Many stress the significance of relationships within the family during childhood, especially with the same-sex parent. Martin Hallet, director of True Freedom Trust, a Christian ministry offering help to Christians struggling with homosexuality[55] has noted that most of the male homosexuals he has counselled felt the lack of an intimate bond with their father or any other significant male figure in early life.[56] Relationships with the peer group in childhood and adolescence may also be significant.

Those who feel different from, or rejected by their same sex peers, can develop an intense desire to be accepted by them. This desire might then become sexual after puberty, with individuals experiencing particular attraction to those who most conform to the ideal of how they themselves would like to be.

However, no one theory of causation fits every individual. It seems best to recognise a "multi-causation model". One writer has concluded, "this would mean that the form and strength of each person's same-sex desire has a distinctive, perhaps unique, mix of biological and psychological factors, and it may be better to speak of 'homosexuali*ties*' ".[57]

How does God view homosexuality?

Those who experience same-sex attraction often suffer from low self-esteem and assume that if others knew about their feelings they would reject them. Christians can be especially sensitive because of the frequent condemnation of homosexuality in some churches. Many begin to sense that they would not only be shunned by their fellow believers if their homosexual feelings became known but that God also disapproves of them, simply because of their desires. But that is certainly not true.

Perhaps you feel that no-one understands you; you do not really understand yourself. But God understands; he knows you better than you know yourself. As the Psalmist wrote, "O Lord, you have searched me and you know me. You know when I sit and when I rise; you perceive my thoughts from afar" (Ps. 139:1–2).

God knows everything about you, even your most secret thoughts and shameful deeds, and yet, amazingly, he still loves you. He did not wait for you to conform to a particular type or standard before he took the initiative to save you. "God demonstrates his own love for us in this: while we were still sinners, Christ died for us" (Rom 5:8). If you are trusting in Christ you can be sure that God is your Father and that you are his much loved child. You can say with Paul, "I am convinced that neither death nor life, neither angels nor demons, neither the present nor the future, nor any powers, neither height nor depth, nor anything else in all creation, will be able to separate us from the love of God that is in Christ Jesus our Lord" (Rom. 8:38-39). God is not ashamed of you. He knows your sins and weaknesses and yet he still delights in you and longs to lavish his love on you. "You are not an unwanted child".[58]

Although God loves those who are attracted to the same sex he does not approve of homosexual practice. We are not to feel guilty or condemned because of our temptations, whether homosexual or heterosexual, but nor should we express them sexually, except in heterosexual marriage. The Bible's consistent teaching is that homosexual practice is wrong. This does not simply rest on a small number of isolated texts, but rather flows out of God's plan for creation as outlined in Genesis 1 and 2. Before looking at the texts that specifically mention homosexuality we need to place our discussion of this issue in the context of the essential building blocks of a Christian worldview: creation, fall, redemption and new creation.

A Christian Worldview

Creation

From the very beginning God differentiated between the sexes: "God created man in his own image, in the image of God he created him; male and female he created them" (Gen. 1:27). We are not simply human beings; we are men and women. Adam is created first and then God says, "It is not good for the man to be alone. I will make a helper suitable for him" (Gen. 2:18). The helper God creates is not another man, but a woman. "Adam is not given a mirror-image companion, he is given a *her*, and he delights in her *correspondence* to him (Gen. 2:23), which resides both in her likeness (human) and her difference (female). The pair are literally and figuratively made for each other".[59] Once he has created our complementary sexuality God then institutes marriage as the proper context for its sexual expression: "For this reason a man will leave his father and mother and be united to his wife, and they will become one flesh" (Gen. 2:24).

Contrary to popular belief, the Bible is not against sex. It begins with a very positive affirmation of our sexuality, as male and female, and of marriage. All the Bible's negatives about alternative contexts for sexual expression flow from these positives of God's creation design. Those negatives certainly do not focus either exclusively or especially on homosexual sex. Scripture affirms sex within marriage and forbids it in every other context, heterosexual or homosexual.

Fall

While Genesis 1 and 2 describe God's perfect design for his creation, the next chapter explains its corruption. When man and woman turn away from God, sin enters the world and corrupts every aspect of our personalities, including our sexuality. We remain in God's image but that image has been marred. Our humanity is now derived, not just from creation, but also from the Fall.

Those who have only been conscious of homosexual desires sometimes argue, "God made me this way; it's natural for me. And, because they are part of my nature, these desires must be good and can therefore be expressed sexually". But in this fallen world it does not follow that an instinct is part of God's design just because it feels natural to me. Just as my selfish and aggressive urges come from the Fall, not God's perfect creation, so many of my sexual urges are also a product of sin. That is true of all of us. Everyone is perverted sexually since the Fall. We all have a desire for sex outside its God-ordained context of marriage and we are all called to resist those desires. None of us has done that perfectly, so there is no excuse for any of us to look down on others in this area. We have all sinned sexually, whether our desires are heterosexual or homosexual.

Redemption

If we are to form a Christian understanding on any subject we should think of the perspective, not just of creation and the Fall, but also of redemption: the salvation Christ has made possible through his death and resurrection. How does Christ's saving work affect our understanding of sex and sexuality?

It is true that the New Testament never records Jesus as referring explicitly to homosexual behaviour, but that does not mean he was neutral on the subject. He clearly endorses the positives of Genesis 1 and 2 which are the basis of the Bible's consistent position that sex outside marriage is wrong. When asked a question about divorce he replies, "Haven't you read . . . that at the beginning the Creator 'made them male and female,' and said, 'For this reason a man will leave his father and mother and be

united to his wife, and the two will become one flesh'?
So they are no longer two, but one. Therefore what God
has joined together, let man not separate" (Mt. 19:4–6).

The New Testament affirms God's creation design by
speaking positively about sex within marriage and negatively about it in all other contexts. Its condemnation of
homosexual practice can not be dismissed as only relevant
to the culture of the time and therefore no longer applicable today. Its roots lie, not in any particular culture, but in
God's plan for creation in all places and at all times.

We should not leave Matthew 19 without noting that,
alongside his affirmation of God's creation plan for sex
and marriage, Jesus also strikes a radically new note by
speaking positively about singleness: "some are eunuchs
because they were born that way; others were made that
way by men; and others have renounced marriage
because of the kingdom of heaven. The one who can
accept this should accept it" (Mt. 19:12). Singleness is
"given" by God (v11), not just to those who have deliberately chosen it for the sake of his kingdom, but also to
those whose circumstances, whether from birth or later
experience, have prevented them from marriage. This
will include some with a homosexual orientation.

Singleness should certainly not be seen as second best.
Jesus never married and never experienced sexual intercourse, but he was the most fully integrated human being
in history. The apostle Paul even teaches that, in some
senses, singleness is "better" than marriage because of
the comparative freedom it can give us in serving Christ
(1 Cor. 7:25–40). Of course there are struggles associated
with singleness, but that is also true of marriage. Paul
speaks of each as a "gift" of God (1 Cor. 7:7), by which he
means singleness or marriage itself, not the ability to be
contentedly single or married. Rather than focussing on
what we find difficult in our circumstances, we should

thank God for whichever gift he has given us and seek to make the most of its advantages. Some single people will later receive the gift of marriage, and some who are married will later receive the gift of singleness again, after divorce or bereavement. Neither state is more spiritual than the other and both are viewed very positively in the New Testament.

New Creation

Christ will one day return to complete his work of salvation and introduce a perfect new creation. Our perspective will change if we live now with that glorious future in mind. There will be no human marriage (Mk. 12:25), but nor will anyone be lonely. All God's people will delight together in the perfect intimacy of our relationship with Christ. The book of Revelation describes his coming as a wedding day when he and his people will be joined together (19:7; 21:2–4). It will be hard to be faithful to Christ in the struggles of this life, including homosexual temptation, but the battle will not continue forever. Any loneliness or frustration we experience now will be replaced by an infinitely greater joy in the future.

Biblical Passages

There are relatively few Bible passages that directly address the subject of homosexual behaviour. This is not the place for a detailed study of them[60] but I will make a brief comment on each. We should remember that they emerge from the broader theological context we have just considered, which sees heterosexual marriage as the only proper place for sex in God's creation design.

Genesis 19 (and Judges 19)

Genesis 19 is the account of the destruction of Sodom and Gomorrah. Angels visit Lot at Sodom and are invited to stay with him. When they hear of their presence, the men of the city surround the house and call to Lot, "where are the men that came to you tonight? Bring them out to us so that we can have sex with them" (v. 5). The traditional interpretation, reflected in the word "sodomy", is that homosexuality is the sin which prompted God to destroy Sodom. But this is reading too much into the passage, and into an account of a similar incident in Judges 19. The sin the rabble threatens is gang rape, which is obviously unacceptable whether it is heterosexual or homosexual. These passages should not be used to argue against homosexual sex in general.

Leviticus 18:22 and 20:13

God's law states that homosexual sex is "detestable". That sounds clear enough, but does this prohibition still apply to God's people today? Some argue that the law in Leviticus is not condemning homosexual sex in general but only homosexual acts in the setting of idolatrous worship. But the context of these laws does not support such a restrictive reading. These chapters cover a range of sexual taboos including adultery (18:20), intercourse with close relatives (18:6) and bestiality (18:23) and are not limited to sexual practices in pagan worship.

But we should still be cautious before we apply these laws today. Leviticus also tells us that we should not eat pork, but that does not stop Christians from eating bacon sandwiches. On what basis can we say that one law still applies and another does not? Thankfully God does not leave us to our intuition alone. The New Testament makes it clear that some laws no longer apply because they were designed only for the old covenant period, which has now been fulfilled in Christ. The food laws, for example, were intended to mark out the racial people of God, the Israelites, as distinctive in the world. They are no longer appropriate now that God's people are a multi-racial, multi-cultural family of those who are in Christ, and so Jesus abrogated them (Mk. 7:19; Acts 10:15). But a law, such as the prohibition against homosexual practice, that is rooted in a creation principle (and is therefore not specific only to one era) and is repeated in the New Testament, still applies to Christians.

Romans 1:26–27

Paul is exposing the sin of the pagan world in their suppression of God's truth and preference for idolatry: "They exchanged the truth of God for a lie, and worshipped and served created things rather than the Creator" (1:25). As a result, God expresses his judgement by "giving them over" (vv. 24, 26 and 28) to the behaviour that follows from their rejection of him. This is manifested in many different sins (see vv. 29–31) including homosexual behaviour: "God gave them over to shameful lusts. Even their women exchanged natural relations for unnatural ones. In the same way the men also abandoned natural relations with women and were inflamed with lust for one another" (1:26–27).

It has been argued that Paul is not condemning all homosexual sex in this passage. He only condemns those who abandon "natural" relations with the opposite sex and so, some say, his words do not apply to those whose natural instincts are homosexual. Others go further and remind us that Paul was a first century Jew and that, therefore, when he refers to homosexuality he inevitably has a first century Jewish notion of what it involves. In the Jewish mindset homosexuality was a Gentile sin which often involved pederasty, as older tutors had sex with younger boys, and took place in idol temples. Paul's condemnation of homosexuality, it is argued, does not say anything about the loving consensual sex that takes place today within committed partnerships of those who are homosexual by nature.

These revisionist readings of Romans 1 do not do justice either to the immediate context of Romans 1:26–27 or the broader context of biblical theology. Paul's theme in this section is creation (1:18-20). When he speaks of "nature" he is not referring to modern understandings of sexual orientation. Homosexual practice is "unnatural", or "against nature" as Paul expresses it, because it goes against God's creation pattern for sex outlined in Genesis. His comments may speak into one particular first century context, but their application is not limited to that context. Homosexual practice is "against nature" wherever it takes place, whether in the context of idol worship or a committed relationship.

1 Corinthians 6:9–10 (and 1 Timothy 1:9–10)

Paul lists ten types of behaviour which, if continued and not repented of, will result in exclusion from the kingdom of God. Two of the words are related to homosexuality. The first is translated "male prostitutes" by the NIV. The word Paul uses can simply mean "soft" or "gentle" but the fact that it appears here, sandwiched between two words that have a sexual meaning, strongly suggests he is using it in a similar sense. It was sometimes used to

refer to boy prostitutes, which is how the NIV understands it. It may be that is too specific a translation and
that Paul is using the word in one of its other senses to
refer to men who deliberately make themselves attractive to other men, or, more specifically, to those who are
the passive partners in homosexual sex.

The other word Paul uses, translated "homosexual
offenders" in the NIV, is a composite word which literally
means "those that lie with men". The same word is used
in 1 Timothy 1:10 (translated "perverts" by the NIV). Some
argue that its meaning should be restricted, for example,
to those who have sex with prostitutes or to pederasts, but
if Paul had such specific behaviour in mind he would
surely not have used a general word (*arsenokoitai*).

It is likely that *arsenokoitai* is a translation into Greek of
two Hebrew words in Leviticus 18:22 and 20:13 ("lying
with a male")[61] which refer to homosexual intercourse in
general. It may be that Paul uses it to refer to the active
partners in homosexual sex.

Even if Paul's primary reference is to particular forms
of homosexual behaviour, there is no reason to believe he
would have condoned it in any other context. The Bible
is entirely consistent on the subject; homosexual practice
is only ever mentioned negatively. It is seen as a depar-
ture from God's creation design for sex, as described in
Genesis 1 and 2 and affirmed throughout Scripture.

Some truths to remember

1. The gospel is liberating

The Bible does not only contain God's challenging standards; it also proclaims many glorious truths that help us
to obey them. If we focus on our weaknesses, temptations

and sins, we will soon lose heart; but Scripture directs our attention to God and his gospel. "The gospel offers 'gay liberation' by breaking the power of sin".[62]

Having listed a variety of forbidden behaviours, including homosexual practice, Paul continues: "And that is what some of you were. But you were washed, you were sanctified, you were justified in the name of the Lord Jesus Christ and by the Spirit of our God" (1 Cor. 6:11). It seems that some members of the church in Corinth had previously been practicing homosexuals, but had since been converted and repented of their sin. They could be sure, as we all can if we have turned to Christ, that they had been completely cleansed of their sin, were fully acceptable to God and righteous in his sight. We do not have to be slaves to our past: "If anyone is in Christ, he is a new creation; the old has gone, the new has come!" (2 Cor. 5:17).

The gay movement appeals to those who experience same-sex attraction to "come out" and publicly accept a homosexual identity. But the path to Christian maturity lies in recognising that our true identity is in Christ and that we are defined by our relationship to him, not by our sexuality. We will grow in humanity and discipleship as we grasp the full wonder of our salvation and live out its implications. The ethical teaching of the New Testament is never simply a list of dos and don'ts but rather flows out of God's saving work for us and in us. Before exhorting the Colossians to "put to death whatever belongs to your earthly nature: sexual immorality, impurity, lust, evil desires and greed" (3:5), Paul grounds his appeal in their new status in Christ: "You have been raised with Christ . . . you died and your life is now hidden with Christ in God. When Christ, who is your life, appears then you also will appear with him in glory" (3:1–4). We do not have to search for acceptance, love and identity; those elusive realities have all been given to us by God's grace in Christ. "Thanks be to God for his indescribable gift!" (2 Cor. 9:15). Now, by the Spirit, we are called to live in the light of our salvation.

Our behaviour will not always live up to our new identity in Christ. When we fail, however drastically, we must resist the devil's lies that we are no longer acceptable to God or that we are too weak to resist temptation and might as well give in to it. Instead, we should turn to God's word and be encouraged by the truths of the gospel. We will be spurred on to keep trying to live for Christ as we are reminded of the three tenses of salvation: "I have been set free from the *penalty* of sin because Christ died for me. I am being set free from the *power* of sin because of the Spirit's work in me. And one day, when Christ returns, I will be set free from the very *presence* of sin." With such a hope we can always say, "our present sufferings are not worth comparing with the glory that will be revealed in us" (Rom. 8:18).

2. Suffering is expected

There is great joy in the Christian life, but Jesus also promised hardship. Alongside the wonder of "knowing Christ and the power of his resurrection" we are also called to the "fellowship of sharing in his sufferings" (Phil 3:10). Some of the sufferings associated with Christian discipleship are common to us all; others depend on our circumstances and personalities.

It is sometimes argued that it is unreasonable to expect Christians with a seemingly fixed homosexual orientation to be denied the privileges of marriage and sexual intimacy and that, therefore, the church should recognise committed same-sex partnerships. But the fact that it is hard to obey God's word does not legitimise disobedience. We sympathise with a husband, for instance, when his wife is afflicted by an incurable condition which makes sexual intercourse impossible, but we do not encourage him to visit prostitutes or to divorce and remarry. In this fallen world some people are called to be faithful to Christ in very difficult circumstances.

We may be right to pray for a change of circumstances, but we must recognise that may not be God's will. We will often struggle to understand God's purposes, but we can be sure that he is in control and lovingly over-rules throughout our lives for our good. James writes in his epistle, "consider it pure joy, whenever you face trials of many kinds" (1:2). He is not encouraging a form of Christian masochism. We are not expected to rejoice at the suffering in and of itself, but rather at the way God purposes it for our good: ". . . because you know that the testing of your faith develops perseverance. Perseverance must finish its work so that you may be mature and complete, not lacking anything" (1:3–4).

William Still, a great and wise Scottish pastor, encouraged those who experience same-sex attraction to trust it to Christ "with a view to seeing how he will re-channel its desire, if intractable, towards something to be used by God. It could then become as beautiful as the fruit of those to whom the gift of natural union is given". God has used such people greatly, for example, "not only in the realms of artistic endeavour, but in those of loving relationships, especially in the befriending and helping of needy souls". He concludes, "some people hold up their hands in holy horror at even hearing that so and so has such a problem. But if they knew how sympathetic the Lord is to the affliction, and how he stands ready to use it when it is given to him, they might be shocked out of their self-righteousness".[63]

3. Change is possible

Although God has not promised to remove our struggles, there is no doubt that many have testified to the fact that God has either completely removed their homosexual feelings or significantly reduced them. Many have experienced such feelings for a short period in their youth but then found that they disappeared. For this reason young people should not be urged to "come out" or even think of themselves as homosexual before they become adults.

Same-sex attraction that continues into adulthood is unlikely simply to disappear with the passing of time, as it can do with teenagers. However, while some have seen little or no change in their sexual orientation, others have found their homosexual feelings diminish or even vanish, usually after much prayer and support, and their heterosexual feelings grow, so that they are ready for relationships with the opposite sex.[64]

The approach of Dr Elizabeth Moberly has been influential in recent years.[65] She advocates a twin approach of prayer and the development of close but non-erotic relationships with people of the same sex. These relationships may then have the effect of shifting the blockages caused, she believes, by unmet needs for same-sex love in childhood, and enable the development of heterosexual desire. One man who has been helped by this approach writes of the transforming effect of a friendship with "an older man who totally banished my fear of father-figures". Over a period of time, he continues, "I found myself becoming steadily more straight than gay, and that has continued until now", although he admits to having "occasional weak patches".[66]

Christians should be both realistic and optimistic about the possibility of change. We must remember that the Bible does not promise that our temptations and struggles will be removed in this fallen world. It may be that we will have to fight the same battles throughout our lives. God has the power to change our sexual orientation, but he may not do so. And yet, even if he does not, we can be sure that, if we look to him, his Spirit will give us the strength to resist temptation and grow in godliness. God is at work in all our lives, changing us into the people he wants us to be: "we, who with unveiled faces all reflect the Lord's glory, are being transformed into his likeness with ever-increasing glory, which comes from the Lord, who is the Spirit" (2 Cor. 3:18).

4. Friendship is vital

Our battles in the Christian life will be infinitely harder if we seek to fight them alone. All of us crave for intimacy: to know and be known, to love and be loved. Without close Christian friends who understand us and accept us, we will find it harder to resist the temptation to satisfy our longings for intimacy in potentially damaging and sinful ways. David Field has written, "If you are a Christian with a homosexual orientation, you have probably experienced the loneliness of relationship-starvation already. You may very understandably have found yourself gravitating toward the gay scene, not because you want casual sex but because you need to find friends who will not shuffle their feet awkwardly when you talk freely about your most intimate desires and concerns. Perhaps you have already reached the point where you divide the week between Christian activities and gay clubs in the half-guilty hope that your two worlds will never meet. This is a split-minded 'solution' that can never work out satisfactorily in the long run".[16]

Our society, and too often our churches, can give the impression that true intimacy can only be found in a sexual relationship and that single people are therefore bound to be lonely. But it is not true that intimacy must involve sex. The Bible describes the deeply affectionate relationship of David and Jonathan (1 Sam. 20:17, 41; 2 Sam. 1:26) and speaks of John as "the disciple whom Jesus loved" (Jn. 13:23; 19:26–27; 21:20). Despite claims to the contrary, there is absolutely no hint that either friendship was sexual.

If you have never shared your homosexual struggles with another Christian, you are missing out on the help you need. Pray that God would enable you to build some deeper friendships in which you can be open with one another and a mutual source of encouragement in the different challenges you all face as you seek to follow Christ.

Close same-sex friendships are often the subject of speculation in our sex-obsessed society. You will need to be honest and wise, especially when sexual feelings are aroused, but you should not be wary of developing deep friendships simply because of the fear of what others may think. This is an area in which the church should be challenging the unhelpful attitudes of the world. "Christian onlookers should resist the train of thought: friendship = gay = homosexual activity. We can be of most help by assuming the best and allowing friendships to blossom".[68]

A challenge to the churches

1. Renounce prejudice

Christians are right to object when anyone who argues that homosexual sex is wrong is dismissed as "homophobic". Many of those who believe the Bible forbids homosexual practice are warmly affirming and supportive of those who have homosexual feelings. Nonetheless, we should recognise that sinful homophobic attitudes do exist in our churches. Our conversation and the tone of our public comments sometimes reveals a dislike, not just of homosexual sin, but of homosexual people. Lance Pierson's words challenge us all to examine our attitudes and to think about the impression our words and actions may give. He writes, "Homophobia is far more widespread than homosexuality. It is not recognised as a pathological condition, so it is largely untreated and unconfessed. Yet those with gay feelings instantly detect it. It wounds them, hammering into them that they are unlovable, unforgivable, unwelcome. We drive them away from our churches, especially evangelical churches, where they assume that they will be condemned. We distort their view of God by implying that he shares our hate of gay people. Our passing remarks and sweeping generalisations in favour of 'a hard line against gays' force many silent sufferers into the misery of secret loneliness".[69]

2. Don't compromise on truth

Love demands an understanding and compassionate response to those who are attracted to the same sex, but it does not justify a compromise in Christian standards of sexual morality. The clear teaching of scripture, as understood by Christians for 2000 years, forbids homosexual practice. We often hear the voice of homosexual Christians who argue for a revisionist reading of the Bible and a liberalisation of the church's ethical teaching. But we should not forget that there are many believers, largely hidden, who also have homosexual feelings but, in obedience to Christ and his word, do not believe it is right for them to engage in homosexual activity. Their struggle to live holy lives is greatly undermined by those who advocate or tolerate a lowering of biblical standards in this area.

One Christian, who had lived a promiscuously homosexual lifestyle before his conversion has written, "it causes many of us profound distress and hurt to witness the extraordinary spectacle of spiritual leaders charged with feeding or ruling the flock of God apparently encouraging same-sex practices . . . The last advice that any of us redeemed homosexuals need to hear in our daily battles is that, in certain circumstances, the deeds that are 'natural' to us are permissible after all! . . . In this delicate area there is a real danger that 'little ones' who believe in Jesus are caused to sin".[70]

3. Live as God's family

We are right to affirm the Bible's prohibition of homosexual sex, but we dare not do so without also ensuring we make every effort to provide the necessary support to enable those with homosexual feelings to live godly lives. There is an important place for trained counsellors and specialist ministries but, above all, churches can help simply by being what they are called to be: the family of God in which brothers and sisters grow together into maturity in Christ. John Stott has written, "at the heart of the homosexual condition is a deep loneliness, the natural human hunger for mutual love, a search for identity and a longing for completeness. If homosexual people can not find these things in the local church family, we have no business to go on using the expression".[71]

Single people can feel as if they are on the fringes of church life. A friend of mine once attended a church

which called its young adults group, "Pairs and Spares".
We may avoid such awful language, but many of our
churches can give the impression that single people are
"spares" who do not fully belong. We should do all we
can to build affectionate, caring relationships across the
spectrum of the church: young and old, single and married, people from different backgrounds and with different personalities. In such a church those struggling with
homosexual temptation, or any other sexual temptation,
will begin to find an emotional fulfilment which will
significantly reduce their craving for sex. They will experience, at least in part, a reflection of the love and acceptance God has already lavished on them in Christ.

8

Keeping Spiritually Fresh

³⁶*Now one of the Pharisees invited Jesus to have dinner with him, so he went to the Pharisee's house and reclined at the table. ³⁷When a woman who had lived a sinful life in that town learned that Jesus was eating at the Pharisee's house, she brought an alabaster jar of perfume, ³⁸and as she stood behind him at his feet weeping, she began to wet his feet with her tears. Then she wiped them with her hair, kissed them and poured perfume on them.*

³⁹*When the Pharisee who had invited him saw this, he said to himself, "If this man were a prophet, he would know who is touching him and what kind of woman she is – that she is a sinner."*

⁴⁰*Jesus answered him, "Simon, I have something to tell you."*

"Tell me, teacher," he said.

⁴¹*"Two men owed money to a certain moneylender. One owed him five hundred denarii, and the other fifty. ⁴²Neither of them had the money to pay him back, so he canceled the debts of both. Now which of them will love him more?"*
⁴³*Simon replied, "I suppose the one who had the bigger debt cancelled."*

"You have judged correctly," Jesus said.

⁴⁴Then he turned toward the woman and said to Simon, "Do you see this woman? I came into your house. You did not give me any water for my feet, but she wet my feet with her tears and wiped them with her hair. ⁴⁵You did not give me a kiss, but this woman, from the time I entered, has not stopped kissing my feet. ⁴⁶You did not put oil on my head, but she has poured perfume on my feet. ⁴⁷Therefore, I tell you, her many sins have been forgiven – for she loved much. But he who has been forgiven little loves little."

⁴⁸Then Jesus said to her, "Your sins are forgiven."

⁴⁹The other guests began to say among themselves, "Who is this who even forgives sins?"

⁵⁰Jesus said to the woman, "Your faith has saved you; go in peace."

Luke 7:36–50

A lavish devotion

It was a big day for Simon. He had managed to persuade Jesus to come to dinner with his friends. Jesus had already established quite a reputation as a preacher and healer, so it was something of a coup to get him to agree. The chefs had been working for hours producing the very best Palestinian food and the guest list was a "Who's Who" of the religious hierarchy in Jerusalem; all the top rabbis had been invited. Everything started well. The guests were charmed by Jesus; he was excellent company. And everyone congratulated Simon on the food and the wine; the Chateau Capernaum went down especially well. But then the pleasant atmosphere was shattered by a commotion in the hall. A disheveled woman rushed through the door, followed closely by the servants who had tried to stop her. It was obvious she had not been invited. No self-respecting Pharisee would be seen dead talking to someone like her. She was known throughout the town as a "sinful woman"; it is possible she was a prostitute.

Simon was furious. How dare she storm in uninvited! The evening had been ruined. And he was horrified when the woman went straight to Jesus, the honored guest, and started weeping. Her tears landed on his feet and she wiped them with her hair before pouring expensive perfume on them. Simon's friends murmured nervously. They had never seen anyone do that at a dinner party before; it was a most embarrassing display. But no one doubted the emotion that lay behind her actions. She clearly loved this teacher very much.

This woman has been a model for followers of Jesus ever since. It was she, the disreputable gate-crasher, rather than Simon, the religious Pharisee, who had understood what Christianity is all about. Simon had greeted Jesus with a cold formality when he had arrived at his home but, by contrast, she was lavish in her devotion to him.

"Do you love Jesus?"

An elderly friend in our church telephoned me one day. "Good morning, Vaughan," she said, "I just wanted to talk to someone about Jesus. Do you love Jesus?" "Yes I do," I replied, "but not as much as I should." "I *love* Jesus," she said, with great emphasis. She meant it. Despite her very tough life, her whole demeanor, even her face, radiates with love for him. Her example is both an inspiration and a challenge to me.

The language of devotion was common in previous Christian generations. One great man of God sometimes began to pray by saying, "Lord Jesus, we come to thee as lovers of thine."[72] Very few of us speak like that these days. We think of the Christian life more as a race and a fight than as a relationship of love, although the New Testament uses all those terms. We tend to speak of "serving the gospel," "knowing the truth" and "loving the word." But, above all, the Christian life is about Christ: being served, known and loved by him and then, in response, serving, knowing and loving him.

I was humbled recently when I was asked to speak at a conference on devotional life. Who was I to speak on that subject? It has always been a struggle for me to maintain a close walk with Christ and I was feeling particularly dry spiritually at the time, but I agreed to give the talk in the hope that it might do me good. I spoke with some friends as I began to prepare. All of them said that keeping spiritually fresh was one of the greatest struggles in their Christian lives, but that they had received very little teaching on this subject. It became clear to me that I should include a chapter on the theme in this book, which I was planning at the time. What follows is the substance of the talk that I gave. The experience of preparing and delivering it was a much-needed personal spur to grow in spiritual discipline and devotion. I wish I could say that I have maintained the progress I made then but, as always, my experience has fluctuated since. Through writing these pages I have renewed my resolve to keep working and praying for a deeper love for Christ and closer walk with him. I hope reading them will have the same effect on you.

This chapter considers six ingredients for a healthy devotional life:

1. Keep an open Bible
2. Be ruthless with sin
3. Think much of Christ
4. Pray often
5. Make the most of other Christians
6. Maintain a regular "quiet time"

1. Keep an Open Bible

"As real as a human friend"

A friend of mine reached for a history book from a high library shelf. As he pulled it out, a piece of paper fluttered to the floor. Intrigued, he picked it up to see what it said and read these words: "Jesus Christ can be as real to you as a human friend." That is gloriously true. Although Jesus Christ lived and died two thousand years ago, he rose from the dead and can be known today. He calls individuals to himself by his Spirit through his word: "My sheep listen to my voice; I know them, and they follow me" (Jn. 10:27).

It was shortly before my eighteenth birthday when I first began to read the Bible seriously for myself. I began with Matthew's Gospel and, to my surprise, I was gripped by what I read in a way that I had never experienced before. I soon had a strong sense that I was not reading ancient words of purely intellectual interest, but rather living words of profound truth. I knew that Christ was real and that he was God. I had a deep conviction that I had to follow him and my life could never be the same again. It was as if he walked off the pages and into my life. The great words of Charles Wesley proved true for me: "He speaks, and, listening to His voice, New life the dead receive."[73]

I heard the voice of Jesus say
"Come unto me and rest;
Lay down thou weary one, lay down
Thy head upon my breast."[74]

All Christians can testify to the same experience in their lives. You may not have had a Bible open like me, but at some time the truth found in Scripture was explained to you and the Holy Spirit enabled you to believe it and trust in Christ. It may have been years ago, as you were growing up in a Christian home or going to Sunday school; or perhaps it was as an adult. It may have been a quick and dramatic experience or it could have been a gradual process over a period of time. Everyone's testimony is different, but there is a common thread running through each one: God calls people to Christ by his Spirit through his word.

"Crave pure spiritual milk"

Having reminded us that we have been born again "through the living and enduring word of God" (1 Pet. 1:23), Peter urges us to continue to hunger for that word: "Like newborn babies, crave pure spiritual milk, so that by it you may grow up in your salvation, now that you have tasted that the Lord is good" (1 Pet. 2:2–3). We need God's word – not just to draw us to Christ in the first place, but also to build us up in our knowledge and love of him.

One of the most notable changes in my life after my conversion was my attitude to the Bible. Previously I had thought of it as a dull, dead book from an ancient world. It made little sense to me and seemed to have no immediate relevance for my life. But, having turned to Christ, I discovered the truth of the Bible's own statement about itself: "the word of God is living and active. Sharper than any double-edged sword" (Heb. 4:12). God had given me an appetite for his word. The school Christian meeting, with its short talk from Scripture, became the highlight of my week. I listened intently. Although over twenty years have passed, I can still remember some of the talks as if they were yesterday. I started going to a Bible study group, even though I was busy revising for some important exams. We studied Romans, which was stretching for a young Christian, but thrilling too. I also began to try to put aside time for personal Bible reading with the help of some notes a teacher had recommended. The study passage for the first day was from Ezekiel 34, a part of the Old Testament I had not even heard of before, let alone read, but I found that Jesus was there too, as he had been in Matthew's Gospel in the New Testament. That great chapter, with its promise of a coming "good shepherd," is still one of the passages I love best.

I wish I could say that the "craving" for the "pure spiritual milk" of God's word that marked my very early days as a Christian has been a constant experience ever since. But there have been periods when I have felt little or no desire to read the Bible and have done so infrequently. It is no coincidence that these have also been the times when I have felt furthest away from God.

A healthy spiritual diet

We are increasingly paying great attention to our physical diet, making sure we have enough of the right vitamins and our five servings of fruit and vegetables each day. Do we show the same concern for our spiritual diet? Are we getting enough Scripture? We should do all we can to join a church where the Bible is faithfully taught and commit ourselves to attending regularly if at all possible. We should also make the most of other opportunities to study the Bible, whether on our own or in groups.

While the challenge for some readers of this chapter is to increase their intake of Scripture, the battle lies elsewhere for others. Some of us listen to plenty of sermons, attend regular small groups and make time for personal Bible reading, but it often feels more like a duty than a joy and we seem to receive little spiritual benefit. What can we do to counter that dryness and bring life to our study of God's word? Here are some suggestions that have helped me.

Always pray first

Without God's help the Bible will remain a closed, dead book, so I must use the key of prayer and ask God by his Spirit to open up its treasures and bring it to life. Every time I turn to the Scriptures, whether on my own, in church, or with others, I should pray with the psalmist: "Open my eyes that I may see wonderful things in your law" (Ps. 119:18). It may be that the preacher at church and the leader of our small group are not especially skilled but, instead of grumbling, we should pray: both for their teaching and for our reception of God's word. God will not turn us away empty if we come to his word with a prayerful hunger.

Keep a varied diet

Rather than letting ourselves get stuck in a rut, we should do all we can to vary our intake of Scripture. Sometimes I find taking careful notes during sermons and my own Bible reading helps me to concentrate and remember what I learn. Then, after a while, it can feel too academic, so I stop writing or simply try to jot down one truth or challenge that has struck me. There have been periods when, perhaps with a friend, I have learned a verse each week. God still recalls to my mind verses I learned years ago to bring a timely rebuke or encouragement. If you are used to reading short passages of Scripture, why not try a quick survey of a longer section for a change? Perhaps you need to go a bit deeper than usual, and study a commentary or take a correspondence course?[75] Or it may be that you need to take a rest from detailed study and simply delight in a familiar passage from the Psalms or the Gospels.

Remember that the Bible is a relational book

When I study Scripture I must remember that I am not just approaching a text to interpret, but a person to encounter. Of course, I should take care to understand it correctly, paying attention to the context and applying the other basic rules of biblical interpretation, but that is not enough. We need to take warning from Jesus' rebuke to the Jewish religious leaders: "You diligently study the Scriptures because you think that by them you possess eternal life. These are the Scriptures that *festify* about me, yet you refuse to come to me to have life" (Jn. 5:39–40).

The Bible is, above all, a relational book. We could see it as a love letter from Jesus. Whenever we open the Bible we should be asking: "What is Jesus telling me about himself in this passage?"

Put it into practice

Both the wise and foolish may hear God's word, but only those who also "put it into practice" are likened by Jesus to the "wise man who built his house on the rock." The others, who hear only but do not obey, are like the foolish builder whose house was built on sand and "fell with a great crash" when the storm came (Mt. 7:24–27).

Jesus said: "If you love me, you will obey what I command" (Jn. 14:15). Our relationship with Christ cannot remain as a warm glow in our hearts; we must express it through obedience. He tells us in his word how to live in a way that pleases him. If we ignore or forget what he says, our relationship with him is bound to go cold. We need to make the effort not just to understand Scripture, but to obey it. One leader of a Bible study group I attended always ended our meetings by asking: "What one truth or challenge are we going to take away from this passage and ask God to help us apply to our lives?" That is a good question to ask whenever we open the Bible.

2. Be Ruthless with Sin

The dangers of unconfessed sin

As we saw in Chapter 3, on guilt, Psalm 32 speaks of the wonder of knowing God's forgiveness. But David had not always enjoyed that experience. At one time, although he knew God, he had resisted him and not confessed his sin or repented of it. As a result, he felt utterly miserable:

> When I kept silent,
> my bones wasted away
>   through my groaning all day long.
> For day and night
>   your hand was heavy upon me;
> my strength was sapped
>   as in the heat of summer
>
> Psalm 32:3–4

Only later did he return to his senses and come clean before God. Then, at last, the relief of God's forgiveness flooded in once more:

> Then I acknowledged my sin to you
>   and did not cover up my iniquity.
> I said, "I will confess
>   my transgressions to the LORD" –
> and you forgave
>   the guilt of my sin.
>
> Psalm 32:5

All Christians know from experience that nothing is more damaging to our relationship with Jesus than unconfessed sin. It is not that sin changes his love for us. We may fall into a terrible sin tomorrow, and yet God will not love us any less. If we have trusted in Christ, God's love for us is absolutely secure. By dying in our place Christ has paid the penalty for all our sin: past, present and future. But, while sin does not change God's love for me at all, it does change my experience of his love for me.

It all begins with a lapse into sin. I have told myself that I will never commit that particular sin, or never do it again, but then I do. The damage to my spiritual health could be limited if I would only turn immediately to Christ, confess my wrongdoing and ask for help to resist temptation in the future. But the devil does all he can to stop me doing that: "You don't really think that God will welcome you back after you've done that, do you? You should hang your head in shame and keep your distance from him rather than presuming to approach him." Once I fall for that tactic, he tries another: "The warmth of your relationship with Jesus has gone. You've let him down and you feel wretched. You've blown it already, so it really doesn't make any difference if you do the same thing again." If I believe that lie, a second sin soon becomes a third, then a fourth. That makes me feel even guiltier and even less inclined to approach God. A vicious cycle has begun and the old warmth of my relationship with Christ has soon been replaced by a coldness. The longer it continues, the harder it is to do what David did: leave the darkness and return consciously into the light of God's presence, saying those words which we all know are so hard to say, "I'm sorry." Only then will I begin to bathe again in the refreshing wonder of God's love and forgiveness.

What is your spiritual Achilles' heel?

If I am to enjoy to the full the wonder of the relationship with God that Christ has secured for me, I must be ruthless with sin. That will mean taking every possible practical step to stop myself from falling into it in the first place. We are all especially vulnerable in different ways. What is your particular Achilles' heel? You could identify it by asking the question, "If I were the devil, where would I direct the attack against myself to try to lead me into sin?" It will probably not be a difficult question to answer. We know where the battle of temptation rages most fiercely when we are tired, lonely, depressed or facing some spiritual challenge. If we are wise we will make sure we give ourselves special protection in those areas. There may be certain places we should not go, people we should not see and lines of thought we should not even begin to explore because of where they might lead.

Sometimes, sadly, I will fall – but I must be ruthless with sin even then. I must not listen to the devil's lies as he tries to persuade me to keep away from Christ and repeat the sin. Instead I should confess right away: "Lord

Jesus, I am sorry." We should develop a regular pattern of confession, acknowledging our sins before the Lord each day. As the old saints used to say, we should "keep short accounts with God." That is not so we can be forgiven. Our forgiveness does not depend on our confession of every single sin we commit. That would be impossible; we often sin and are not even aware of it. I am to confess not so I can secure my forgiveness, but rather so that I can experience again the wonder of the forgiveness Christ won for me on the cross.

3. Think Much of Christ

Much of our spiritual instability stems from spending too much time focusing on ourselves: our actions, feelings and circumstances. Instead, we need to focus on Christ: his work, promises and love. We should heed the call of the writer to the Hebrews: "Let us fix our eyes on Jesus" (Heb. 12:2).

Christ's work, not my conduct

When we stop to think about it, we know that our relationship with Christ depends not on what we do for him, but on what he has done for us. We are not saved by works but by God's grace as we trust in Christ. But we quickly forget this fundamental truth when we think about our relationship with God. We focus too much on how we are doing in the Christian life. If we manage to resist temptation, we are on a high; but if we fall, we feel low. If we have a good time of Bible reading and prayer, we are sure we are close to God; but if we forget to open the Bible for a day or two, we convince ourselves that we are far from him. As a result, our spiritual barometers are always going up and down. Instead, we should be focusing on Christ's work.

The woman who anointed Jesus is a good model to follow. Jesus said of her: "her many sins have been forgiven – for she loved much" (Lk. 7:47). He did not say, "I have forgiven her because she has shown me such love." That would have contradicted the little parable he told Simon, the host at the party (Lk. 7:41–43). Jesus spoke of two men whose debts were cancelled by a moneylender. He then asked Simon which of them would love the lender more: the one who owed five hundred denarii, or the one who owed fifty? The answer is obvious: "the one who had the bigger debt canceled." Jesus then pro- ceeded to speak of the woman and her extravagant display of love towards him. Her love did not secure her forgiveness. Rather, she expressed her love out of gratitude for the forgiveness she had already received by grace.

God's love precedes ours: "We love because he first loved us" (1 Jn. 4:19). We must keep thinking about Christ and his death for us through which we are completely forgiven, and then we respond with a love of our own. We should daily thank Christ for the cross and acknowledge our constant dependence on what he has done for us. And we should make the most of the Lord's Supper which he provided for our benefit until he returns. As we take the bread and wine we remember his sacrifice for us and, in the words of the Anglican Prayer Book, "feed on him in our hearts by faith with thanksgiving." We will be praising Christ for his death in eternity, singing "Worthy is the Lamb, who was slain" (Rev. 5:12), but we should not wait until heaven to do that. The cross is to be the central theme of our worship here on earth, both in song and in the offering of our lives to his service.

See from His head, His hands, His feet,
Sorrow and love flow mingled down!
Did e'er such love and sorrow meet,
Or thorns compose so rich a crown?

Were the whole realm of nature mine,
That were a present far too small;
Love so amazing, so divine,
Demands my soul, my life, my all.[76]

Christ's promise, not my feelings

Some people are emotional yo-yos, whose feelings are always fluctuating up and down. Others are prone to depression; their feelings may be down, down, down and only occasionally up. Whatever our personalities, we should make sure that we anchor our spiritual lives in Christ's promises, not our feelings. Our feelings often change, but Christ's promises remain eternally secure. We may not sense his presence, but he has said: "surely I am with you always, to the very end of the age" (Mtt. 28:20). We may at times even feel abandoned by him, but we can be sure he is still with us. He has guaranteed that "whoever comes to me I will never drive away" (Jn. 6:37).

One member of our church was suffering from severe depression and said to a former pastor as she left the church, "I just can't believe it." Very wisely he replied, "Facts not feelings, Daphne." She told me years later how those words had often sustained her through hard times. She knew the facts; she knew Jesus was the Son of God who had died for her, been raised and would return. And she knew that he promised to forgive all who turn to him and to live with them through the Holy Spirit. She relied on those facts and the solid dependability of Christ's promises, not her fluctuating moods.

We live in an experiential age, but we should resist the urge to chase experiences in our Christian lives. Some go to church looking, above all, for an experience. If they have what a friend of mine calls a "liver shiver," an experience that somehow takes them out of themselves, they leave encouraged and sensing that God is present and does love them. But what happens when that experience wears off on Monday morning at the office? And how do they cope when they are nowhere near that large congregation with the excellent music group and latest sound system? They may not experience the same feeling quite so often in a church that may be faithful, but is small, meets in a cold building and depends for its music on a tentative organist playing an out-of-tune instrument.

Charles Spurgeon once said, "I looked at Christ and the dove of peace flew into my heart; I looked at the dove and it flew away." Of course our relationship with Christ should affect our emotions, but we should not look to them for our security. Spiritual highs come and go, but Christ and his promises never change. "Jesus Christ is the same yesterday and today and forever" (Heb. 13:8).

Christ's love, not my circumstances

All of us will face difficult periods in our lives. Our faith does not protect us from illness, loneliness, bereavement, unemployment or broken relationships. At times we may suffer to such an extent that we even wonder whether God cares, but we can be sure that he does. Paul writes: "For I am convinced that neither death nor life, neither angels nor demons, neither the present nor the future, nor any powers, neither height nor depth, nor anything else in all creation, will be able to separate us from the love of God that is in Christ Jesus our Lord" (Rom. 8:38–39).

My friend Daphne, who suffered from depression for many years, used to start every day by singing a hymn. She would wake us up at church conferences by singing her daily hymn in the corridor. That regular pattern of praise gave her the perspective that enabled her to cope with much hardship in her life. Whatever trials we may have to endure, there is always much we can thank God for, not least his eternal love for us in Christ.

I once interviewed Arthur, another former member of our church who is now with Christ in heaven, about his experience of bereavement. In a short space of time his wife, son, daughter and grandson had all died. But he had no trace of self-pity. "God has been so good to me," he insisted, and his radiant face made it obvious that he meant it. He was not denying the reality and pain of grief, but through that dark suffering he had kept his eyes fixed on the light of Christ.

Someone once told me, "For every look within, take ten looks at him." I have never thought that is quite enough. Perhaps it should be "one hundred looks at him." The health and stability of our Christian lives depend on thinking much of Christ.

4. Pray often

"Pray continually"

All relationships, including our relationship with God, depend on two-way communication: he speaks to us through the Bible and we speak to him as we pray. The apostle Paul encourages us to "pray continually"

(1 Thess. 5:17). We are not limited to set times and places. We can pray all the time, wherever we are and whatever the circumstances.

When we have a close friendship with someone, we want to share our life with them. If something amusing, frightening or surprising happens we think to ourselves, "I can't wait to tell him or her." Wonderfully, we never have to wait to speak to Jesus; he is always with us. So when we see a beautiful sunset we can say immediately, "Thank you, Lord." If we are faced with a sudden temptation we can cry out, "Help, Lord." After falling into sin we can confess quickly, "I'm sorry, Lord." And if we face a difficult decision and need wisdom we can ask, "Please, Lord."

It's time to pray

It is always a privilege to get to know godly older Christians for whom prayer is as natural as breathing. They can be talking to you one moment and then, almost before you notice, they slip quite naturally into talking to their heavenly Father. That spiritual maturity takes a lifetime to develop. Most of us can go for hours without even thinking of Christ, let alone speaking to him. One friend of mine tried to prevent that from happening by resolving to pray every time he got onto his bicycle, which he does many times every day. That provided the trigger that helped him to enjoy more regular conscious fellowship with Christ. Another friend who was leading a university mission encouraged the Christian students to put a small sticker on their watches. He suggested that they pray for a non-Christian every time they saw the sticker: "What's the time? It's time to pray!"

STOP!

There is great value in setting aside time for concentrated prayer in addition· to making the most of the opportunity to pray brief prayers throughout our daily lives. I still often follow the pattern that I was first taught as a young Christian: STOP.

Sorry: We should develop a pattern of regular confession of sins.

Thank you: It's so easy to rush through life without ever pausing to remember all that the Lord has given me and is doing for me. Even when life is difficult I always find that there is much that I want to thank him for once I stop and think.

Others: There may be a few people we will want to pray for daily; others less frequently. I have found a prayer list helpful, with some names under each day of the week. I have often been unrealistic in drawing up the list with the result that my prayers degenerate into a quick "God bless Tuesday's group." It is best to keep the list short and to keep adapting it.

Please: This is the section for personal prayers. Of course it is right that we take all our concerns before our heavenly Father in prayer. Nothing is too small or insignificant for his concern. But my prayers for myself should not only focus on my practical daily needs; I should also be praying for growth in godliness and Christian maturity.

Keep adapting

My prayer time can quickly become a dull routine in which I merely say the words without much conviction or sense of relationship. I have to keep adapting my approach to counter that tendency. I may use "STOP" for a while before making a change and basing my prayers around the different phrases of the Lord's Prayer. I have also found it helpful to write out some daily prayers, partly based on particular challenges I have recently received from God's word. That ensures my prayers have some substance and continuity. As I keep praying the same requests for a while I am able to look out for the answers. I also use the prayers of others at times and make them my own: whether prayer from the Bible, especially Paul's, or from great Christians of the past. There are tremendous spiritual riches, for example, in the Anglican Book of Common Prayer or in a wonderful collection of Puritan prayers called *The Valley of Vision*.[77]

Pray with others

I was nervous when I was invited to my first prayer meeting. For a while I did not have the confidence to pray myself and was worried that if I began a prayer I would not be able to complete it. A friend helpfully suggested that I might like to write down a prayer in advance and read it out. Even then I was worried that I might start to speak just as someone else was beginning to pray. I am pleased I persevered. I have learned more about prayer in prayer meetings than anywhere else as I have observed the model of others: not just the words they use, but their faith, devotion and perseverance. Corporate prayer has also enabled me to pray for much longer and with greater concentration than I can by myself. Prayer meetings are the spiritual powerhouses behind many works of God.

5. Make the Most of Other Christians

The New Testament understands Christian growth as something that must take place, above all, not individually, but corporately. We are not to be lone rangers who try to grow to maturity in Christ on our own. Christians are brothers and sisters in a family and members of a body. Paul tells the Ephesians: "speaking the truth in love, we will in all things grow up into him who is the Head, that is, Christ. From him the whole body, joined and held together by every supporting ligament, grows and builds itself up in love, as each part does its work" (Eph. 4:15–16).

Just as individual parts of a body, like an arm or a leg, cannot function without being connected to the other parts, so each Christian needs to be joined to others in a church. The New Testament assumes that our membership of a church will not be limited to occasional attendance. We will need to build close relationships if we are to give and receive what we should. That may take time and effort, but it will pay rich dividends.

I owe a huge amount to my church family. Some pray for me every day. I will only know in heaven what a difference that has made. Others spur me on by their godly example. Their perseverance, sometimes through extreme suffering, challenges me to press on despite any troubles I may be experiencing. Many offer friendship, hospitality and encouragement. Ours is certainly not a perfect church, but the people have often shown the love of Christ to me and been used to strengthen me in my relationship with him. Christians who remain on the fringes of church life miss out on so much.

We should take care to develop close Christian friendships. Many of us find that we talk with one another about cricket, Christmas, and even croquet, far more than we talk about Christ. There should be those who can ask us occasionally, "How's your walk with the Lord?" Christian couples should ensure that they pray together regularly and are open with one another about their spiritual lives. Many have found prayer partners or triplets a spur to continued prayer and a context in which deeper friendships can grow. They may also provide the trusting relationships which enable us to open up, share our struggles and be accountable in areas of particular temptation.

6. Maintain a Regular "Quiet Time"

"Next to love for the Lord Jesus"

Stephen Neill was a theologian, a bishop in India, a missionary statesman, and he wrote dozens of books. A student asked him in later life how he had managed to accomplish so much. "Discipline," he replied. "Oh," said the young man, "I was afraid you might say that." Neill continued, "Next to love for the Lord Jesus, discipline is the most important quality in the Christian life."

Each of the ingredients for a healthy devotional life that we have considered so far in this chapter requires discipline. I want to close by commending one in particular, which some Christians have called a "quiet time": a few minutes set aside every day for Bible study and prayer. There has perhaps been a danger of legalism in the past. The Bible does not lay down any laws in this area – nor should we. But many, like me, have found great value in the practice.

"Seven Minutes with God"

Habits developed early in life tend to stick, for good or ill. I am grateful for those who encouraged me as a young Christian to get up slightly earlier in the morning and spend time with the Lord. One pastor used to hand out a leaflet called "Seven Minutes with God." It suggested starting with one minute of prayer, asking God by his Spirit to speak through his word. Then it suggested spending four minutes reading a short passage of Scripture, then two minutes of prayer at the end. It was wise advice. Seven minutes probably sounds manageable for those who have never tried a quiet time before. Any longer could put them off from trying. In time, most people decide that they want to extend the period.

Spending time with God early in the morning works best for me, but you may prefer a different time. Routine tends to help. If I wait for a spare moment, it rarely comes. I need to set aside a few minutes in my daily timetable. The best time may change as circumstances vary. A young woman who may have been used to spending forty minutes with God early in the morning may be wise to settle for twenty minutes later in the day after the birth of a child. If we miss days we should not be gripped with guilt. Rather, we should simply start again the next day.

We should pray that our regular times of Bible study and prayer are not simply a duty but a joy, as we delight in conscious fellowship with God. As I turn to the Bible, I should remember that I am not reading an academic textbook. I am a son listening to my loving heavenly Father; a sheep hearing the voice of the shepherd.

I was not helped in the early days of my Christian life by an impression I had received that I could expect to hear a direct message from God for the precise circumstances of my life every time I read the Bible. That left me discouraged, as my morning passage often seemed to have little immediate relevance to the particular personal issue with which I was grappling on that day. But the Bible was not written directly to me. It is not a collection of lots of little messages waiting to be applied by the Spirit to the detailed circumstances of my life. I cannot expect to be "zapped" by a directly applicable word from the Lord from its pages every time I read it. It was a great relief when a friend pointed this out and told me that, rather than containing a series of particular messages for me the Bible, above all, contains great truths about God. He suggested that, instead of focusing on myself and my immediate concerns as I read the Bible, I should concentrate on God and ask myself, "What is this passage teaching me about him?" As I grow in understanding of the Bible's teaching about God and his plan of salvation I will see more and more clearly that those great truths have implications for every detail of my life.

Spiritual nuggets to delight in

We should be conscious of God's presence with us as we read his word. As well as praying as we begin for help in understanding, we can pray throughout our times of study. Every great truth we discover, or challenge we receive, can prompt an immediate prayerful response of adoration, confession or intercession. Some sections of the Bible immediately yield spiritual nuggets to delight in; other sections require more digging or reflection. Whatever the passage, it can be helpful to focus on one "best thought" to remember and take away for meditation and application. We might write it down and refer to it again later. If we can transfer our quiet time into portable form, it will benefit us throughout the day and not just for a few minutes.

While there is great value in the discipline of a routine, it can take us into a rut if we are not careful. As mentioned above, I have to keep changing my pattern of prayer and Bible study so my time with God stays fresh. I am not naturally disciplined in this area and have to battle to maintain a regular quiet time, but I know it is a battle worth fighting. Maintaining my walk with Jesus through life depends as much on those few precious minutes each day as on anything else.

Strength for the Battle

Paul tells the Ephesians, "our struggle is not against flesh and blood, but against the rulers, against the authorities, against the powers of this dark world and against the spiritual forces of evil in the heavenly realms" (Eph. 6:12). The devil is at work in all the battles we face and in ourselves we are no match for him. So we must be "strong in the Lord and in his mighty power" (Eph. 6:10).

As the woman in Luke 7 knew, the Christian life is, at heart, a loving relationship with Jesus who first loved us and died for us on the cross. No one course of action will guarantee an ongoing vibrant relationship with him for the rest of our lives, but applying these six principles will bring rich fellowship with God and vital spiritual resources for the struggles of this present world until, at last, we can say with the apostle Paul: "I have fought the good fight, I have finished the race, I have kept the faith" (2 Tim. 4:7). When Christ appears, all our insecurities, lust, guilt, doubt, depression and pride will disappear forever. And there will be no unfulfilled spiritual longings on that day for we will see Christ "face to face" and know him as we are fully known (1 Cor. 13:12).

Endnotes

[1] Quoted in D. Tidball, *That's Life!* (Leicester, UK: IVP, 1989), p. 107.

[2] Mike Starkey, "Who Am I?", *CPAS, CY Magazine* 7 (www.cpas.org.uk; Dec. 1997), p. 13.

[3] *London Sunday Times* (7 Jan. 2001).

[4] Quoted in S. James, *God's Design for Women* (Darlington, UK: Evangelical Press, 2002), p. 259.

[5] N. Wolf, *The Beauty Myth* (London: Vintage, 1991), p. 10.

[6] *London Times* (24 May 2005).

[7] *London Times* (7 Nov. 2005).

[8] Wolf, *The Beauty Myth*, p. 289.

[9] Quoted in M. Starkey, *Fashion and Style* (Crowborough, UK: Monarch, 1995), p. 174.

[10] Starkey, *Fashion and Style*, p. 162.

[11] R. Valerio, "If the Shoe Fits, Don't Buy It!" *Idea Magazine* (Nov./Dec. 1999), pp. 30–32.

[12] G. MacDonald, *When Men Think Private Thoughts* (Nashville, TN: Thomas Nelson, 1996), p. 4.

[13] James, *God's Design for Women*, p. 259.

[14] Starkey, "Who Am I?" *CPAS, CY Magazine*, p. 14.

[15] *New Musical Express Student Guide* (2000).

[16] J. Stott, *The Contemporary Christian* (Leicester, UK: IVP, 1995), p. 157.

[17] J. Harris, *Not Even a Hint* (Sisters, OR: Multnomah, 1993), pp. 18–19.

[18] J. Piper, *Future Grace* (Sisters, OR: Multnomah, 1995), p. 336.

[19] E. D. Wilson, *Steering Clear* (Leicester, UK: IVP, 2002), p. 10.

[20] Wilson, *Steering Clear*, p. 22.

[21] T. L. Eisenman, *Temptations Men Face* (Downers Grove, IL: IVP, 1990), p. 54.

[22] P. Yancey, *What's So Amazing About Grace?* (Grand Rapids, MI: Zondervan, 1997), p. 35.

[23] J. C. Winslow, *Confession and Absolution* (London: Hodder, 1960), p. 22.

[24] From Ben Elton, *Popcorn*, quoted in N. Pollard, *Why Do They Do That?* (Tring, UK: Lion, 1998), p. 112.

[25] *London Times* (17 May 2005).

[26] *London Times* (1 Aug. 1999).

[27] Charles Wesley, "And Can it Be that I Should Gain?"

[28] O. Guinness, *Doubt: Faith in Two Minds* (Tring, UK: Lion, 2nd edn, 1983).

[29] Guinness, *Doubt*, p. 19.

[30] R. Dawkins, *The Selfish Gene* (Oxford: Oxford University Press, 2nd edn, 1989), p. 198.

[31] D. H. S. Nicholson and A. H. E. Lee, *The Oxford Book of English Mystical Verse* (Camarillo, CA: Acropolis Books, 1997).

[32] J. Stott, *The Cross of Christ* (Leicester, UK: IVP, 1986), p. 312.

[33] Guinness, *Doubt*, p. 162.

[34] Guinness, *Doubt*, p. 113.

[35] Quoted in Guinness, *Doubt*, p. 113.

[36] Guinness, *Doubt*, p. 67.

[37] C. S. Lewis, *The Screwtape Letters* (London: Fontana, 1974), p. 35.

[38] A. McGrath, *Doubt* (Leicester, UK: IVP, 1990), p. 111.

[39] C. Williams, *I'm Not Supposed to Feel Like This* (London: Hodder, 2002).

[40] M. Wilcock, *The Message of the Psalms 1–72* (The Bible Speaks Today; Leicester, UK: IVP, 2001), p. 155.

[41] It is possible he was a prisoner of war. We know from 2 Kings 14 that King Jehoash of Israel attacked the southern kingdom of Judah and took hostages from Jerusalem back to the northern kingdom.

[42] C. S. Lewis, *A Grief Observed* (London: Faber and Faber, 1973), p. 9.

[43] A. Dallimore, *Spurgeon* (Edinburgh: Banner of Truth, 1991), p. 186.

[44] Roger Carswell, "Treasures of Darkness: Depression – A Personal Point of View," *Evangelicals Now* (Oct. 2005).

[45] M. Lloyd-Jones, *Spiritual Depression* (Basingstoke, UK: Pickering, 1965), pp. 20–21.

[46] J. Piper, *Tested by Fire* (Leicester, UK: IVP, 2001), p. 109.

[47] G. Davies, *Genius and Grace* (Tain, Scotland: Christian Focus, 2005), p. 221.

[48] C. S. Lewis, *Mere Christianity* (London: Fontana, 1952), Ch. 8, p. 106.

[49] G. M. Marsden, *Jonathan Edwards: A Life* (Yale: Yale University Press, 2004), p. 225.

[50] A. Dallimore, *George Whitefield*, II (Edinburgh: Banner of Truth, 1990), p. 353.

[51] Isaac Watts, "When I Survey the Wondrous Cross."

[52] Kinsey, A. C., Pomeroy, W. B., Martin, C. E., *Sexual Behaviour in the Human Male*, Reprint ed., (Indiana University Press, Bloomington, 1988).

[53] Wellings, K., Field, J., Johnson, A. and Wadsworth, J., *Sexual Behaviour in Britain* (Penguin, London, 1984), p. 187; Laumann, E. O., Gagnon, J. H., Michael, R. T. and Michaels, S., *The Social Organisation of Sexuality: Sexual Practices in the United States* (University of Chicago Press, Chicago, 1994), p. 294, 296, 303.

[54] Stott, J., *Issues Facing Christians Today*, 4th Ed. (Zondervan, Grand Rapids, 2006), p. 445.

[55] True Freedom Trust: www.truefreedomtrust.co.uk.

[56] Homosexuality, *Nucleus* (January 1994), pp. 14–19.

[57] Goddard, A., *Homosexuality and the Church of England* (Grove Books, Cambridge, 2004).

[58] Keane, C., *What Some of You Were* (Matthias Press, London, 2001), p. 29.

[59] Schmidt, T. E., *Straight and Narrow?* (IVP, Leicester, 1995), p. 44.

[60] Gagnon, R. A. J., *The Bible and Homosexual Practice* (Abingdon Press, Nashville, 2001), is a thorough treatment of the Bible's teaching in this area; Schmidt, T., *Straight and Narrow?* (IVP, Leicester, 1995); Peterson, D. (Ed.), *Holiness and Sexuality* (Paternoster, Milton Keynes, 2004), are excellent introductions.

[61] Wright, D., *Homosexuals or prostitutes? The meaning of* Arsenokoitai (1 Cor 6:9, 1 Tim 1:10, 1984), *Vigiliae Christianae* 38, p. 125-153.

[62] Townsend, C., *Homosexuality: Finding the Way of Truth and Love, Cambridge Papers*, Vol. 3, No. 2.

[63] Searle, D. (Ed.), *Truth and Love in a Sexually Disordered World* (Paternoster, Milton Keynes, 1997), p. 51.

[64] There are a number of Christian ministries which seek to help those wanting to deal with unwanted homosexual feelings including Exodus International (www.exodus-international.org); True Freedom Trust in the UK (www.truefreedomtrust.co.uk) and Liberty Christian Ministries Inc. in Australia (www.libertychristianministries.org.au).

[65] Moberly, E., *Homosexuality: A New Christian Ethic* (Clarke, Cambridge, 1983).

[66] Pierson, L., *No-Gay Areas?* 3rd Ed (Grove Books, Cambridge, 1997), p. 19.

[67] Field, D., *Homosexuality: What Does the Bible Say?* Rev, Ed. (UCCF, Leicester, 1998), p. 36.

[68] Pierson, L., *No-Gay Areas?* 3rd. Ed. (Grove Books, Cambridge, 1997), p. 24.

[69] Pierson, L., *No-Gay Areas?* 3rd. Ed. (Grove Books, Cambridge, 1997), p. 7–8.

[70] Searle, D. (Ed.), *Truth and Love in a Sexually Disordered World* (Paternoster, Milton Keynes, 1997), pp. 55–56.

[71] Stott, J., *Issues Facing Christians Today*, 4th Ed. (Zondervan, Grand Rapids, 2006), p. 476.

[72] J. Eddison, *Bash: A Study in Spiritual Power* (Basingstoke, UK: Marshalls, 1982), p. 42.

[73] Charles Wesley, "O for a Thousand Tongues to Sing."

[74] Horatius Bonar, "I Heard the Voice of Jesus Say."

[75] The Open Bible Institute (incorporating the Moore College Correspondence Course) is especially recommended. For further details go to www.open-bible-institute.org.

[76] Watts, "When I Survey."

[77] A. Bennett, *The Valley of Vision* (Edinburgh: Banner of Truth, 1975).

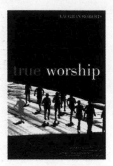

True Worship by Vaughan Roberts

What is the nature of true, Christian worship?
What are we actually doing when we meet together for
'church' on Sundays?

And how does that connect with what we do the rest of
the week? Vaughan Roberts answers these questions and
more as he brings readers back to the Bible in order to
define what worship is and isn't, what it should and
shouldn't be. While we may struggle to define worship
by arguing about singing hymns with the organ, versus
modern songs with guitars, or about the place of certain
spiritual gifts, Roberts suggests we are asking the wrong
questions. For true worship is more than this – it is to
encompass the whole of life. This book challenges us to
worship God every day of the week, with all our heart,
mind, soul and strength.

ISBN 978-1-85078-445-6

Available on www.authenticmedia.co.uk or from your
local Christian bookshop

Turning Points by Vaughan Roberts

Is there meaning to life? – Is human history a random process going nowhere? – Or is it under control, heading towards a goal, a destination? – And what about my life? Where do I fit in to the grand scheme of things?

These are topical questions in any age, but perhaps particularly so in a largely disillusioned postmodern era such as ours. Vaughan Roberts addresses these questions and others as he looks at what the Bible presents as the 'turning points' in history, from creation to the end of the world. This book does not read like a normal history book. No mention is made of great battles and emperors of whom we learnt at school. It will not help you pass exams or score extra marks in a pub quiz. It aims to do something far more important, to help you see history as God sees it, so that you might fit in with his plans for the world.

'Racy and profound, brilliant and biblical, this book is a powerful apologetic and magnet to Jesus Christ.' *Michael Green, Adviser in Evangelism to the Archbishops of Canterbury and York*

ISBN 978-1-85078-336-7
Available on www.authenticmedia.co.uk or from your local Christian bookshop